Portrait of - MANCHESTER

JOHN CREIGHTON

Sigma Leisure - Wilmslow

First published in 1988 by **Sigma Leisure,** an imprint of **Sigma Press** 1 South Oak Lane, Wilmslow, SK9 6AR

British Library Cataloguing in Publication Data
Portrait of Manchester
1. Greater Manchester (Metropolitan County)
Manchester History
I. Title
942.7'33

ISBN: 1 85058 121 5

Acknowledgments: The Author would like to thank the following who provided information and materials for his book:
The City Engineer's Department, Manchester; Documentary Photography Archives; Mirror Group of Newspapers; Manchester Evening News; Manchester Metro News; Chetham's Library; Manchester Grammar School; Library Theatre Company; Manchester Theatres Limited; Manchester City Art Galleries; Free Trade Hall; Manchester Cathedral; Castlefield Urban Heritage Park; G-Mex Exhibition and Event Centre; Manchester Museum of Science and Industry; Granada TV Limited; The British Broadcasting Corporation; Greater Manchester Buses Limited; Rochdale Canal Company; British Rail; Manchester International Airport; Manchester United FC; Manchester City FC; Lancashire County Cricket Club; Samuel Websters and Wilsons Ltd; Greenwood Tighe PR; Marks and Spencer; C and A Modes Ltd; Holiday Inns (UK) Ltd; Yang Sing Restaurant; Britannia Hotel; Refuge Group Plc; Midland Bank Plc;

Front Cover Picture: Piccadilly in its heyday - the shopping centre of Manchester, bustling with trams and buses.

Contents

December 1900 at the junction of New Cannon Street and Market Street

Mancunians pose for the photographer in August 1900. Corporation Street is on the right where a horse-drawn cart is full of coal.

1. Introduction

History and Development

Manchester, one of Europe's principal cities, is mainly a creation of the 19th and 20th centuries. There are, however, many reminders of earlier times including part of a Roman fort, a 15th century cathedral and a variety of elegant 18th century houses.

The site at the confluence of the Rivers Irk, Medlock and Irwell was ideal for a Roman fort. Built of timber and earth in the first century AD, it was replaced the next century by a structure with stone ramparts. The stone fort was occupied for some 200 years until 410 AD when the Roman military occupation ceased. About half a century later the area was populated by Anglian and then Danish invaders. Northumbrian Angles and the descendants of Viking invaders lived in the region prior to the Norman Conquest, and the Domesday Book states that Roger de Poitou granted part of Salford Hundred (including the very large manor of Manchester) to Albert Grelley, whose family held the Barony of Manchester for the next two centuries.

How did Manchester acquire its name? Its origins are probably found in the Roman 'Mamucium' or 'Mancunium'. Anglo-Saxons referred to their 'burgh' as 'Mameceaster' and the final version of today's name only became popular in the 1600s.

Manchester became a baronial borough in 1301, still under the control of the lord of the manor but with a boroughreeve or mayor. During the 14th century the manor was held by the de la Warre family, and Thomas de la Warre, in 1422, founded a college and a collegiate church, which later became the cathedral.

Manchester supported Parliament in the Civil War and the town withstood a Royalist siege in 1642. But in 1715 there were Jacobite riots in Manchester and when Prince Charles Edward Stuart entered the town in 1745 he found considerable Jacobite support.

The mid-18th century saw the rise of the cotton industry. 1781 brought the opening of the town's first cotton mill by Sir Richard Arkwright. Trade was boosted in the 18th and 19th centuries by the construction of canals and railways, the Ship Canal making Manchester the world's first inland port. Manchester became a municipal borough in 1838, and the city played a major part in the Reform Act of 1832. In the 1840s the town became the focus of attention as Cobden and Bright fought for a 'laissez faire' trading policy, non-intervention in foreign affairs and the repeal of the Corn Laws, which they achieved in 1846. The Lancashire cotton famine left its mark on the area in the mid-1860s following the failure of the cotton-crop during the American Civil War.

The slums of the 1900s largely dated from the mid-19th century and replaced rambling 17th and 18th century houses. From the early 1920s onwards efforts were made to rehouse the people from these districts, especially in the newly built houses in the garden city of Wythenshawe, a part of Cheshire bought by Manchester City Council in the late 1920s and incorporated into Lancashire in 1930. German air attacks in 1940 and 1941 destroyed considerable parts of Manchester, so various improvements and new roads changed the face of the city in the 1960s.

Greater Manchester today has a population of some 2.7 million and the city is recognised as a major commercial and cultural area. It offers a fascinating architectural heritage plus a host of leisure activities. Manchester is ideally placed for easy access to North Wales, Snowdonia, the Peak District and Lake District. Coastal resorts of Lancashire are within close proximity while neighbouring Cheshire has much to offer the visitor.

Some Famous Men and Women

Education and Science

Bishop Hugh Oldham founded the Manchester Grammar School in 1515 and Humphrey Chetham's practical interest in education led him to found Chetham's Hospital in the 1650s. Public education in Manchester was greatly assisted by a number of people, including Richard Cobden and Sir James Kay-Shuttleworth. In 1832 he published a report on the moral and physical condition of Manchester's working classes, and championed a need for reform in house sanitation and hours of employment. Kay-Shuttleworth suggested these could be achieved by a general system of education. Manchester was one of the pioneers of higher education in the last century and, in 1851, John Owens had a college commemorated to him. This acquired full university status in 1880.

Famous names of technology, science and mathematics are closely associated with Manchester and its institutions of higher learning. John Dalton can be said to be the founder of Manchester's association with chemistry and he became president of the city's Literary and Philosophical Society. The first Professor of Chemistry at Owens College was Edward Frankland, while James Prescott Joule was mainly concerned with the mechanical equivalent of heat. Much of his work was done in the Manchester area.

Examples of other renowned people associated with the city include Schuster, Roscoe, Chadwick and Rutherford, who received the Nobel prize for chemistry, for his work on the nature of the atomic nucleus.

Media, Arts and Literature

Thomas de Quincey spent his boyhood in Manchester in the late 1700s writing his, 'Vision of Sudden Death' in a Manchester hostelry. The novelist Harrison Ainsworth lived in Manchester in the early 1800s and Frances Hodgson Burnett hailed from the Cheetham Hill Road area. Elizabeth Gaskell was not a native of Manchester but she knew the city well and most of her books were written in her Georgian Manchester home. 'Mary Barton' (1848) and 'North and South' described factory life in the city. Engel's book, 'The Conditions of the Working Classes' (1844) was based on Manchester and its environs.

The city was also the home of famous musicians, including Charles Hallé, Hans Richter and John Barbirolli, the Hallé Orchestra's principal conductor. The Whitworth Institute was set up following a gift from the legatees of Sir Joseph Whitworth and the John Rylands Library was built, equipped and endowed by Mrs. Rylands as a memorial to her husband (see 'John Rylands Library' in Chapter 2).

Trade and Industry

Royce of Rolls Royce built his first car in the Hulme district of

Manchester suffered considerable damage during the Second World War.

A 25 foot central reservation on Princess Road was ideal for tram track laid in the mid-1920s. This scene dates from 1944 with the 'Princess Hotel' on the left.

Manchester, and Mather and Platt were internationally famous for their pumping machinery. Beyer and Peacock exported their locomotives throughout the world and, still on the theme of transport, Crossley's motor works had a base in Manchester. Henry Simon sent machinery overseas and Alliott Vernon Roe (AVRO) built bombers in a Great Ancoats Street factory. Sebastian de Ferranti made his home in the city and the Henry family had long associations with the area through chemical manufacturing. Richard Cobden and John Bright have been referred to already. Although not actually residing in Manchester, Arkwright, Crompton, Kay and Cartwright provided a number of ideas and inventions which were greatly appreciated by local industry. In fact, as has been already mentioned, Manchester's first cotton mill was built by Arkwright - his mechanical spinning process was the basis of mass-production in the cotton industry.

Other Important Figures

David Lloyd George was born in the Chorlton-on-Medlock district in 1863, while the inventor of the first general railway time table, George Bradshaw, had an office in Manchester's Brown Street. Aviators John Alcock and Arthur Whitton-Brown are closely associated with the city. They met at the Metropolitan-Vickers factory in Trafford Park and resolved to fly non-stop across the Atlantic. Their epic flight in 1919 was the first Atlantic crossing by aeroplane.

Albert Square and Manchester Town Hall in 1939. As the sand bags and air raid shelters indicate, war has just been declared.

A general view of Albert Square in 1958 - the statues and Town Hall have yet to be cleaned.

2. Architectural Heritage

Manchester offers a wide range of architectural styles from converted Victorian buildings to the Arndale Centre, one of Europe's largest covered shopping areas. A look round Manchester's centre will reveal imposing warehouses now mostly converted to luxury hotels or offices. In addition to these premises, there are impressive public buildings, banks, concert halls and magnificent churches. Manchester has recently experienced an explosion of commercial and public development as instanced by the £1.5m rebuilding of a derelict Victorian block, Albion House. Due to open in 1989, this is another gem in the growing collection of superb restorations in central Manchester.

The Town Hall

Albert Square is dominated by the Town Hall, a brick building faced in sandstone whose exterior provides interesting examples of 13th century style Gothic architecture. Construction began in 1868. Alfred Waterhouse the architect was faced with producing a Town Hall on a site roughly triangular in shape. Waterhouse is also associated with Strangeways Prison (1863), Owens College (1902) and the former Refuge Assurance Company on Oxford Street (1891).

Looking at the Town Hall from Albert Square does not encourage appreciation of the nine years of labour it took to build, and one has to walk round the whole building to do justice to it.

There is an impressive entrance and the large windows of the Mayor's quarters are on the first floor. The huge clock tower is 286 feet high and features an octagonal upper stage.

Visitors are greeted by a vaulted entrance hall. A grand staircase goes up the Great Hall on the first floor. Students of sculpture will have much to admire, particularly the statue of Agricola, the Roman general largely responsible for establishing Mamucium in 79 A.D. There are regular guided tours at the historic Council Chamber and State Rooms for visitors to the Town Hall.

5

The Town Hall Extension on Mount Street is joined to the principal building by two-storey foot-bridges. Designed by architect Vincent Harris, the Extension was opened in 1938, four years after the adjacent Central Library came into existence. The addition to the Town Hall is essentially a simple building in terms of decoration, with a high front section and lines of neat rectangular windows. It acts as a tasteful link between the somewhat elaborate Town Hall and the neighbouring Central Library.

A partially pedestrianised Albert Square allows visitors to enjoy the blend of buildings and statues, including the Albert memorial, designed by Thomas Worthington in 1862. One of Manchester's most renowned Victorian architects, Worthington's other work includes the Crown Court, Minshull Street (1865) (now a crown court), and Nicholl's Hospital (1878).

Central Library

This impressive Portland Stone structure in St. Peter's Square features an imposing five bay Corinthian portico. To fully appreciate the result of Vincent Harris' work between 1930 and 1934 step inside the library. Here one discovers a huge reading room and its large dome. The various departments within Central Library are the Commercial Library and General Reader's Library on the ground floor; Social Sciences Library and Technical Library on the first floor; Archive department on the mezzanine floor; Local History, Jewish and Arts Libraries on the second floor with the Language and Literature Library occupying the fourth floor. The third floor is for staff use only. Interestingly, the Commercial Library's extensive collection of directories is one of the most comprehensive outside London. The Library Theatre is housed in the basement of Central Library and a description appears elsewhere in this book.

John Rylands Library

Opened formerly in January 1900, the building is a tribute to John Rylands who made his fortune in the Wigan textile trade. Mrs. Rylands' association with the library did not cease with its building

The author's photograph of the Town Hall contrasts the old and the new.

An early morning view of the Town Hall Extension (left)

Sunlight catches the Albert Memorial, designed by Worthington. The statue itself is the work of Matthew Noble.

(1890- 1899), since she endowed it with a yearly income for maintenance and extension. In 1901, she announced that the Earl of Crawford's famous collection of illuminated manuscripts had been acquired. Examples of other treasures include a 42 line Gutenberg Bible of 1546, a Caxton Chaucer of 1476, various French Revolutionary pamphlets and the first printed book with music. John Rylands Library also houses the world's best collection of books from the press founded in Venice by Aldus Manutius in 1495.

This Basil Champneys building on Deansgate has become a scholar's library, merging with the University of Manchester Library in 1972 to form the third largest university library in Britain with some 3.5 million books.

The reader is welcomed by a spacious vaulted vestibule. A majestic staircase leads to the main library, 148 feet in length on the first floor. The reading room, 125 feet long, has a magnificent vaulted ceiling. After walking through art nouveau gates, a spiral staircase takes the visitor to the upper galleries. The stone vaulted ceiling is covered by concrete, and large stained glass windows depict luminaries of philosophy, literature, art and theology. There are many fine details on bookcases and door furniture and the library was one of the first buildings in Manchester to use electric lighting.

1988 has brought a certain amount of concern and controversy as a £1m. appeal was launched to preserve this modern Gothic cathedral of learning constructed in pink sandstone. An estimated £76,000 worth of rare books went on sale in Spring 1988, including a copy of St. Augustine's 'The City of God' published in the 15th century. In fact, the sale raised £1,800,000 and proceeds were used to make the collection more accessible to both the people of Manchester and to scholars. Unfortunately, following the sale, the present Earl of Crawford has decided removed the collection from the safe-keeping of John Rylands' to that of the National Library of Scotland in Edinburgh.

The Free Trade Hall

The Anti-Corn Law League, famous musicians and the Hallé Orchestra

Taken just six years after the Central Library was constructed in 1934, this photograph shows that the building was an air raid shelter accommodating 400 people.

A five-bay Corinthian portico greets today's visitor to the Central Library.

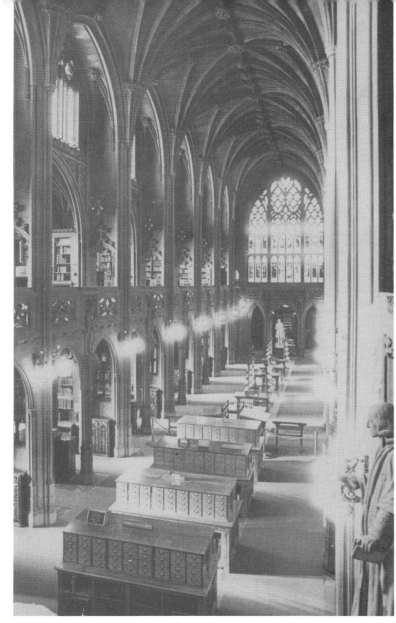

The majestic interior of John Rylands Library is the perfect place to browse through old volumes and manuscripts.

Few public buildings can boast this Classical Italianate style of architecture of the Free Trade Hall.

are just a few famous examples of how the Free Trade Hall has played a prominent rôle in Manchester's history.

During the 1830s and 1840s a campaign against the Corn Laws was launched by the Anti-Corn Law League, whose principal members were Cobden, Bright, Wilson and Charles Pelham Villiers.

A large wooden pavilion was built in 1840 at St. Peter's Fields, the scene of the so-called 'Peterloo Massacre' in 1819. The structure could accommodate between four and five thousand people and it lasted for three years after which it was pulled down and replaced by a brick building.

The first musical event took place in 1843 when John Hullah led 1,500 performers at the first meeting of the Lancashire and Cheshire Workmen's Singing Classes. Gradually musical concerts became an integral part of the Hall's entertainment and 1856 saw the third Hall open on the original site. It hosted political meetings, boxing matches, concerts and even Buffalo Bill when his Wild West Show visited Manchester at the end of the 19th century.

The famous 'Gentlemen's Concerts' engaged Mr. Charles Hallé as a conductor for the orchestra. In 1858 an impressive concert took place which linked this man with the city's fame as a centre for classical music. Hallé made rigorous efforts to bring his concerts to all classes of society by making cheap seats available at his performances. Manchester Corporation purchased the Free Trade Hall from the Public Hall Company in 1921 and it continued to offer an interesting selection of concerts.

The building

Constructed in the 'palazzo' style, the Free Trade Hall's interior and exterior attracted much attention. Unfortunately, on the night of December 22nd, 1940 a bombing raid destroyed everything except two outer walls. It fell to the City Architect, Leonard C. Howitt, to reconstruct the Hall which eventually reopened in 1951.

The exterior is as it was built in 1853 and there are two impressive storeys. The grand storey is an open arcade, while the upper one is an arrangement of pedimented windows and coupled columns. Above this is a highly decorated corniche and a parapet wall.

Manchester Cathedral in the early 1900s. The statue of Oliver Cromwell (right) now stands in Wythenshawe Park.

Built to commemorate the Diamond Jubilee of Queen Victoria in 1897, the Victoria Porch is on the left of this illustration.

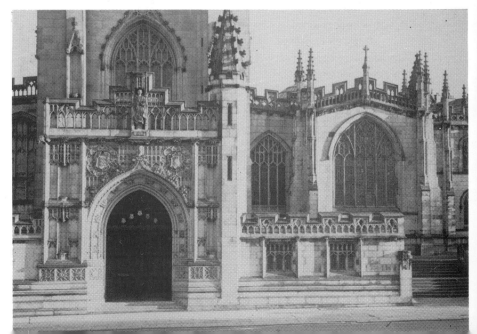

Considerable restoration of St. Ann's Church took place in the late 19th century.

The interior comprises the Large Hall (123 feet by 78 feet), the Lesser Hall, Promenade and Lounge. Decorative features of the Large Hall stem from acoustic requirements and there is seating for 2,900 at public meetings or 2,600 at orchestral concerts.

Today's Free Trade Hall continues with its traditional rôle, offering a wide variety of events. These range from evangelical rallies, trade union meetings to the regular Hallé concerts.

Places of Worship

Manchester has been host to a number of religious groups and here are may examples of churches representing several denominations. Among the city's famous clergymen were the Bishops of Manchester, particularly Bishop Fraser, the second cleric to hold this post.

The Cathedral

The Domesday Book reveals there were two churches in the large manor of Manchester, St. Mary's and St. Michael's. It is likely that the former was one of the predecessors of the present cathedral. St Michael's could be found in the parish of Ashton-under-Lyne, which, although it still belonged to the manor of Manchester, had its own parish church by 1300. Lord de la Warre, priest and lord of Manchester, obtained a licence in 1422 for a collegiate church and it is possible that the building of a new church between the reigns of Henry VI and Henry VII created new buildings in the Fennel Street area. The ancient parish church of Manchester only became a cathedral in 1847 and today its 130 foot tower fights for recognition amidst modern office blocks.

The original structure was largely built between 1421 and 1515, with the choir stalls dating from 1508. The first warden and rector was John Huntington, former rector at Ashton-under-Lyne. Using both old and new materials, he built the choir of the present cathedral with aisles on either side. Later wardens carried on his admirable work. Warden Ralph Langley, for instance, built the nave between 1465 and 1481. The outer aisle originally comprised a ring of chantry chapels whose main function was to provide an altar and a place where clergy would pray for benefactors. These extra areas of worship naturally increased the size of the church. Viewed from the outside, they suggest that there is an outer north aisle and choir aisle and an outer south aisle and outer south chapels.

During the last century, the partitions and screens of the nave chapel were removed and, consequently, little remains of the nave chantries, although those near the choir are still in evidence. So too is the huge choir screen which splits the church into two sections. This imposing wooden screen has panels and doors with intricate carved tracery.

The Lady Chapel screen is the oldest of many such examples in the cathedral, lovingly restored following severe damage by a bombing raid in 1940. Other fascinating sights inside the building include a 1701 silver ewer, 17th century Dutch communion cups, modern stained glass windows and three royal charters from Elizabeth I, Henry V and Charles I.

Restoration work
The cathedral has undergone extensive restoration particularly in 1815 and 1882. The tower was rebuilt during 1887 to the same design as the previous one but with an extra six feet on top of the old height of 124´. The 19th century also brought the construction of the present entrances.

Following the Second World War restoration work was carried out under the direction of Sir Hubert Worthington. A new Lady Chapel was created and roofs were renovated. In 1960, improvements were made in the baptistery, while panels of stone tracery over the entrance to the chapter house have been filled with murals. Improved lighting and more comfortable seating in the nave have enhanced the cathedral's appearance and encouraged visitors to spend more time examining Manchester's principal place of worship.

St. Ann's Church
Much speculation has surrounded the identity of St. Ann's architect. Some people suggest it was Sir Christopher Wren or one of his students. A foundation stone was laid in 1709 by Lady Ann Bland of Hulme Hall, the lady of the manor, the church dedicated to St. Ann in honour of its patroness who provided the biggest financial contribution

Cobden's statue with St. Ann's Church in the background.

St. Matthew's Sunday School features a curved south end wall.

The main entrance to St. Mary's Mulberry Street.

to built it. Lady Ann also supplied a velvet communion table cover and a quantity of silver plate.

Sir Alfred Waterhouse was responsible for the considerable restoration work between 1886 and 1891 and the nave's choir is his work. The building originally possessed a three stage cupola but its poor state of repair necessitated removal in 1777. A spire took its place but this too deteriorated and was in turn superseded by today's tower.

The area covered by St. Ann's church and the square was originally a corn field named Acres Field, the venue for Manchester's September Fair. Gradually, houses were built in the area and these gave way to offices and shops as residents moved to other parts of Manchester.

St. Matthew's Sunday School

A stroll down Liverpool Road from Deansgate will reveal several places of interest, including the 'Oxnoble' pub and Liverpool Road Station. Just after the 'Oxnoble' one comes across St. Matthew's Sunday School. This 1827 building is now used as an office but the original south-west end can still be seen, adding an interesting dimension to the structure.

The church of St. Matthew occupied a site between the market halls on Liverpool Road. Built in 1825 and demolished in 1951, it was designed by Sir Charles Barry who is perhaps best known as the architect of the Houses of Parliament.

St. Mary's, Mulberry Street

Sandwiched between towering buildings, the 'Hidden Gem' lies in a secluded area just off Albert Square. Dating from 1848 and designed by architects Weightman and Hadfield, St. Mary's is a popular place of worship particularly for Catholic office workers. The church does not have the most pleasing façade in terms of architecture but the red brick building features a tower and impressive entrance. The ornate altar and interior marble columns are worth inspecting.

Cross Street Chapel

There is a long history of non-conformist worship on the site from 1694 onwards. The first building was burned down by a Jacobite mob in 1715, and German bombs destroyed the second structure in the Second World War. The third building dates from 1958/59, the work of F. Leslie Hallidav.

3. Places to Visit

Wythenshawe Hall

It seems likely that an earlier house may have stood on the present site. Certainly Robert Tatton was responsible for building a hall in 1540, possibly using materials from the older house. The 17th century structure was in the form of the letter 'H' with a rear courtyard, and today the central section is still timber-framed, possibly dating from Henry VIII's reign.

Extensions were carried out in the late 18th century when Hester and William Tatton resided at Wythenshawe Hall and the Long Gallery was removed to make way for three floors at the southern end of the house. Further improvements were carried out by William Tatton, who continued the family's intention to develop the hall. The famous architect Edward Blore was consulted about modifications in the 1830s, probably recommended to Thomas William Tatton by his cousin, Lord Francis Egerton, for whom Blore carried out alterations on Worsley Hall between 1837 and 1843.

During the mid-1800s a new billiard room was built, extensions added to the dining room, and, in 1871, the North Lodge was constructed. The final phase of the extension on the north end of the hall commenced in 1879 and a three floor extension to the rear staircase was finished in 1895. The hall passed to the City of Manchester in 1926. The central section became a museum while the first floor bedrooms behind the Withdrawing Room were converted into a large exhibition room.

Considerable reconstruction took place between 1947 and 1952 as the extension to the back staircase, front side of the south wing and the conservatory were demolished. Dry rot and beetle infestation in 1978 caused the closure of Wythenshawe Hall until 1983, and today one of Manchester's oldest buildings is open for the public to enjoy such things as the recently discovered Tudor wall paintings and 17th century collections of oak, walnut and inlaid furniture.

A visit to the Hall would not be complete without a stroll through the

14

The 17th Century building at Wythenshawe was H-shaped.

Oliver Cromwell's statue in Wythenshawe Park.

The façade at the former Town Hall is preserved in Heaton Park.

250 acres of parkland which was given to Manchester in 1926 by Lord and Lady Simon of Wythenshawe. They purchased it from R.H.G. Tatton, the last member of the family to own the house. A statue of Oliver Cromwell occupies a prominent position in the grounds opposite the hall. It was removed from its original position outside the Cathedral and placed in Wythenshawe Park partly because it was felt that a statue of Cromwell was too radical for the then conservative politicians. There are facilities for tennis, bowls, and horse-riding. A fine horticultural centre is nearby too with practical demonstrations and lectures by trained staff.

Heaton Hall

Built in neo-classical style, the Hall stands amidst 600 acres of glorious parkland just five miles from the city centre. Heaton Hall was constructed in 1777 by James Wyatt for Sir Thomas Egerton, later the Earl of Wilton. It is arguably one of Wyatt's finest pieces of work.

The original house of 1750 is reflected in the central façade on the north side and here Wyatt's contribution was four Tuscan columns. He designed all the south side plus some lower wings. The Hall comprises just one-and-a-half storeys and the end pavilions have canted fronts. It was acquired by Manchester Corporation in 1902, and today the Hall has much to offer visitors. Its 18th century furniture and paintings are impressive, and the unique Pompeiian Room has been restored in recent years. The original Samuel Green organ is a treat for musical ears and regular musical recitals feature among the Hall's summer attractions.

John Webb and William Ernes landscaped the parkland and the façade of the Old Manchester Town Hall is preserved here. Designed by Francis Goodwin in 1823, it originally consisted of nine bays and was located in King Street.

The grounds at Heaton Park include formal gardens, tennis courts, 18 hole golf course, pony riding and a boating lake. A Farm Centre, is found in the former 18th century stable blocks and a Pets Corner allows animals to be observed at close quarters. Heaton Park also has tram-tracks. People can ride on old trams most weekends. On one September

Sunday every year it is the starting and finishing point of the Heaton Park Bus Rally in which many local bus preservation societies take part with their vehicles.

Platt Hall

This elegant 18th century family home contains one of the finest costume collections in the country. Examples of brocaded and embroidered dress from the 17th and 18th centuries are on show together with the quieter, more sombre clothes of Victorian times.

Platt Hall, built in 1762 as the home of a wealthy textile merchant, is situated in Platt Fields Park, Rusholme. The Gallery of English Costume was opened in 1947 to house the substantial costume collection of Dr. Willett Cunnington, one of the first serious students of dress.

From its inception the collection comprised articles whose value lay in their sociological importance as much as for their decorative qualities. So, the typical garb of Lancashire mill workers has as much to offer as an expensive ballgown. In addition to clothes, the visitor can examine an extensive range of accessories, including handbags, umbrellas and curling tongs. There is a collection of almost 160 dolls together with numerous costume books and old photographs.

However impressive the contents of Platt Hall, the actual building is worthy of inspection. It was constructed for the Worsley family in Georgian style, featuring seven bays and a porch guarded by two pairs of columns. Inside one finds a splendid staircase and interesting plaster ceilings. The Hall does not seem to be affected by time, even though it was once deep in the countryside and is now part of the urban setting.

Fletcher Moss Museum and Art Gallery

Formerly known as the Old Parsonage, Didsbury, the Fletcher Moss Museum and Art Gallery was bequeathed to the city of Manchester by Alderman Moss in 1919. His family bought the parsonage in 1884 and introduced some 19th century Gothic additions.

The majority of the building dates from around 1800, although the central block may date from the early 16th century when it was a

16

Platt Hall stands in Platt Fields Park, Rusholme some two miles south of the city centre.

An interesting view of Didsbury in 1946 with Fletcher Moss Museum and Art Gallery situated in the bottom right-hand corner. The curving Wilmslow Road is clearly visible (centre) and the 'Old Cock' public house occupies a position between the bend and Fletcher Moss.

priest's house. Fletcher Moss contains many products manufactured in Manchester or closely associated with the city. Visitors can admire 19th and early 20th century paintings and the Arts and Crafts room is well worth looking at. Other items of interest include metal work by local craftsman G.F. Armitage and Machmurdo furniture from Pownall Hall, Wilmslow.

In the gardens, one discovers an orchid house, alpine house, delightful herbaceous borders, together with a vast array of unusual trees, shrubs and plants. There is also provision for tennis and bowling, while less energetic people may take refreshments in the Alpine Tea Room.

G-Mex

Older Manchester residents will look at the G-Mex complex and recall its days as a railway station. It is hard to believe that this exhibition centre was a few years ago a sad reminder of urban decay. Central Station closed on Monday, May 5th, 1969. The last train departure was on May 3rd, while the last arrival came in just after midnight on May 4th. It had served Manchester for almost 90 years as the Manchester terminus for the Cheshire Lines Committee Railway. The Cheshire Lines introduced several new routes from Central Station with the Liverpool-Manchester line proving quite popular.

The 1969 closure heralded the end for Central Station and its 26 acres of prime inner city land. Naturally, speculation surrounded its future as vandals and weather took their toll of the buildings. It was not until 1977 that structural repairs saved the station from collapse. The station became an NCP car park meanwhile. Time went by amid discussions about redevelopments until 1978 when the Greater Manchester Council bought the entire 26 acres. In 1980, GMC and Commercial Union announced a year-long joint venture study whose aim was to create a practical solution to the site's development.

As a consequence of this, in 1981 there was news of a decision to convert the listed Train Hall to a national-standard exhibitions and events centre. Following considerable lobbying, the EEC and the Government agreed to provide substantial backing for the £21m. plus scheme. In the summer of 1983, work began on a railway terminus aged just over 100 years.

The alterations

It was decided to retain as much detail and character as possible, not least the 18 massive iron arches carrying the huge single-span roof. So, a design was drawn up reflecting the original structure, with a considerable amount of glazing on each gable end.

The architects created an exhibition hall offering 110,000 square feet of floor space with the facility to divide one/two thirds by means of movable floor-to-ceiling partitions. The old Victorian ironwork had been seriously affected by the weather, so moulds were made from which identical new castings were manufactured. The foundations allowed engineers to increase their size to accommodate nearly 800 vehicles beneath the exhibition hall. Room for a further 1,750 spaces was found next to the Centre.

There is no doubt that G-Mex has much appeal for exhibitors. Its roof is 90 feet above ground level and so presents no height restrictions to exhibitors. Again, the exhibition area is devoid of pillars. During the nine month period from its opening in March to the end of 1986, no less than 27 exhibitions were contracted to take place. In 1987 there was a complete sell-out and the enquiries for the 1990s look most promising.

China Town

A walk around the streets between Piccadilly and Princess Street will take visitors past a huge selection of Chinese restaurants, supermarkets and herbalists catering for the Chinese community in the north west. The magnificent Chinese Archway attracts most attention. Designed by architects from China, it is decorated with gold leaf, lacquer and paints from the orient. An adjacent Chinese garden is a quiet haven in the city centre.

So-called 'China Town' is seen at its best when important events from the Chinese calendar are celebrated. The traditional Chinese lunar calendar has a 60-year cycle which is divided into five sub-sections.

Opened in 1876, the former Central Station was transformed into G-Mex a century or so later. The original roof had a span of 210 feet.

Pictured leaving the Town Hall, this 200 foot dragon makes its way to China Town.

Murals depicting the Roman occupation at the Castlefield area.

Each of these is represented by 12 animal signs. 1988 was the Year of the Dragon and Manchester's China Town celebrated it along with Chinese populations in Hong Kong, Singapore, Malaysia, San Francisco and London. Of course, Manchester's Chinese children are given the opportunity to take part in the various cultural events, including kite making, painting and calligraphy.

Castlefield and the Romans

The name of this area derives from 'Castle in the Field' - a popular 18th century label given to the remains of the old Roman fort. The district was occupied by the Romans led by General Agricola in AD 79 and they stayed for more than 300 years, leaving a stone-built fort.

The original fort was built of turf and timber and stood from AD 79 to about AD 110/125. Since the south side was protected by the Rivers Irwell and Medlock, the two defensive ditches lay on three sides only, with ramparts inside the ditches measuring five metres in height. The fort attracted a civilian settlement of about 2,000 some of whom were involved in manufacturing bronze.

In about AD 160 a large fort was constructed on the site of the first one, accommodating a more substantial garrison than before. Some 40 years later a further fort replaced the turf and timber structure. This stone building was occupied for about 200 years until AD 410 when the Roman occupation of Britain ceased.

In the 16th century, the fort survived as an upstanding earthwork, but during the Industrial Revolution all surface remains of the fort were lost apart from a small section of wall beneath one of the railway arches. So what can today's visitor expect to see at Castlefield in terms of the Romans? The north gateway of the Roman fort has been imaginatively reconstructed on its original site and the guardroom has been equipped as it might have appeared in Roman times. A nearby mural provides an interesting history of Castlefield and is worth viewing.

Castlefield Visitor's Centre provides an introduction to the whole Castlefield area and it has information about visits to the guardroom and excavations. Of course, recently archaeologists have been at work

The north gateway at the Roman fort has been reconstructed on its original site.

in the area and credit has to be given to the efforts of Manchester University and the Greater Manchester Archaeological Unit. During 1988, for example, an excavation team unearthed some bits of pottery depicting scenes of frenzied frolicking. This find came to light as experts dug underneath the arches near Manchester's Roman fort. Although the 1988 discoveries were among the richest found at the site, the excavation team had to move out to allow building to go ahead. Even though the tireless work of archaeologists has increased 20th century understanding of Roman Manchester, a great deal of our past will remain firmly buried in the Castlefield complex.

Murals depicting the Roman occupation at the Castlefield area.

Pictured new in 1903, tramcar number 222 was an open-top vehicle whose maximum fare was two pennies!

This illuminated tramcar with its patriotic message was based at Hyde Road Depot and is shown just before setting off through Manchester in June 1905.

4. Transport

Buses and Trams

The last decade has brought many changes for public transport in Manchester. But when did it all begin? In 1824, Mr. John Greenwood started to operate a one-horse bus service from Pendleton to Market Street, Manchester. Aimed at wealthy business people the fare for this journey was sixpence. A double-decker horse-drawn omnibus made its début in 1852, carrying 42 passengers. Eight years later there were almost seventy omnibuses operating in Manchester. 1865 saw the emergence of the Manchester Carriage Company, and horse trams first came on the scene during 1877 on the Deansgate - Bury New Road route.

Electric tramways changed Manchester's streets as the city opened its system in June 1901. By 1907 there were over 500 electric trams, and routes went as far afield as Audenshaw, Heaton Park, Stretford and Stockport. The last horse-drawn tram was withdrawn from service in 1903.

During the 1920s, central reservations on Kingsway and Princess Road were built solely for trams but people were now looking at the advantages of the motor bus. In 1927 the first express bus service appeared and 1930 saw bus number 189 replace a tramcar. Prior to this, double-decker buses had been found only in the suburbs but in 1930 they were used on city centre routes.

A new distinctive livery was chosen in the mid-1930s as vehicles adopted a streamlined look. Windows were given more graceful curves, Crossley designed a new radiator shell, while improvements were made to the interior décor.

Typical buses on Manchester streets in the mid-1930s included the Crossley 'Mancunian', Crossley 'Alpha' and Leyland Titan TD3s. The 'Alphas' were ordered in May 1934 and featured Metro-Cammell-Crossley B32R bodywork.

Following the war, the streamlined swoops disappeared from buses and the area of cream in the design was reduced. In these years there

21

were some 1,200 motor buses and 153 trolleybuses, gradually leading to the demise of the tram. The last one ran from Piccadilly to Birchfields Depot in 1949.

1950 witnessed the last extension to the trolleybus system, although some critics pointed out the disadvantages of such vehicles. For ,instance, they had to negotiate junctions slowly, overhead wires were often considered an eyesore and one trolleybus could not overtake another. So, in 1952 it was decided that a total motor bus system would be more practical and the conversion to motor bus services occurred.

Manchester trolleybuses included Leyland TB4 chassis models carrying Metro-Cammell-Crossley bodywork. Six-wheelers were popular as typified by those with Metro-Cammell-Crossley bodies and Crossley TDD6 chassis. By 1966 there remained just one trolleybus route on the Manchester-Ashton service and this was converted to motor bus service in December of that year.

Change was certainly in the air during the mid-1960s with one-man buses appearing in 1967 and the following year saw the introduction of the Transport Act. This brought about the end of Manchester City Transport Department in 1969 with the inception of SELNEC (the South East Lancashire and North East Cheshire PTE).

SELNEC placed an order for 500 double-decker buses in 1971. Park Royal supplied 200 bodies, the remainder coming from Northern Counties. Chassis were supplied by Leyland Atlanteans (150 models) and Daimler Fleetline (350 vehicles). Soon buses in the area were painted in the distinctive orange and white livery. Initially, it was quite unusual to see, for example, a former North Western Road Car Company Bristol VR in the new colours but gradually people became used to the new régime. Vehicles from Stockport, Leigh, Oldham Rochdale, Bolton, Bury and S.H.M.D. were eventually repainted and supplied with a SELNEC logo.

In 1974 the responsibilities for public transport were assumed by the Transportation Committee of the Greater Manchester Council, and the PTE became known as GMPTE.

The 1985 Transport Act introduced the complete deregulation of bus services outside London and it had a dramatic effect throughout

AXJ 466, pictured in 1940, is a Crossley 'Alpha' whose life was very interesting. An experimental bus, it was converted to town gas, stored in the bag on the roof, and following the War it became a towing vehicle.

Capable of seating 75 passengers, this SELNEC Atlantean with Park Royal body was acquired in 1971.

A popular sight on Manchester streets, the Little Gem minibus carries 26 passengers. Featuring an Iveco chassis, it measures 6.3 metres in length and 2.2 metres in width.

The Leyland Olympian bus seats 73 passengers and is 9.5 metres long.

Greater Manchester. October 26th, 1986 saw Greater Manchester Buses Limited begin trading and in order to achieve the necessary economies three depots and four engineering workshops had to be closed.

Competition started modestly at deregulation, increasing significantly with the inauguration of the Bee Line Bus Company whose fleet of minibuses appeared on the roads of South Manchester in January 1987. There are now few parts of Greater Manchester which are not covered by a competitive service as routes are run by larger established companies and smaller one- person operators.

The first minibus service to operate in Greater Manchester was implemented in Ashton-under-Lyne in 1986 with subsequent services appearing in Altrincham, Wigan, Bury and Rochdale. These routes were not marketed under a common brand name until the 'Little Gem' identity was launched in February 1987.

Greater Manchester Buses Limited is the leading vehicle operator in the area with over 2,000 vehicles and 6,300 staff. The back-bone of the service is the double-decker bus whose size and carrying capacity make them popular on busy routes. A refinement of double-decker services has been the VHF programme. Very High Frequency routes feed into the commercial centres of Greater Manchester with a guarantee that the next GM bus is only a few minutes away. GM Express routes are popular, while Little Gem minibuses are found on more than 50 routes.

Manchester Light Rapid Transit System was given the go-ahead by Government in 1988, having had its public trials at Debdale Park, Gorton in March 1987. The first £50m. phases of the supertram project will be finished in 1991, linking Altrincham in the south to Bury in the north via Manchester city centre. Trams will operate on tracks receiving their power from overhead power lines. The trams will take up half the road with the remaining highway left free for cars and buses.

The lines will provide a direct link between Victoria and Piccadilly stations. Environmentalists should be pleased to learn that the system is a quick, clean and quiet mode of transport through Manchester centre and it is hoped that it will help change the pattern of travel from cars to public transport.

LRTS has a long planning history in Manchester, from the proposed underground line first out forward in 1901, which was revived in 1936 and rejected in R. Nicholas's *'City of Manchester Plan'* in 1945, through to the 'duo-rail' of the 1960s to the 'Pic-Vic' line of the 1970s.

Railways

Mention railways in the context of Manchester and many people will immediately think of the world's first passenger station at Liverpool Road. Important as this was, one should remember that by the mid-19th century seven railway lines served Manchester, linking it with other centres of commerce like Leeds, Birmingham and Sheffield. For many years, Manchester boasted numerous locomotive works, several engine sheds and numerous large goods depots.

Liverpool Road Station

The Duke of Wellington opened the Liverpool and Manchester Railway in 1830 and it later became part of the LNWR. Liverpool Road was constructed in four months and was used as a passenger station until 1844 when services were moved to the new Victoria station. Liverpool Road carried on as a thriving goods depot until the mid 20th century. British Rail later sold the station and it was used to house the Museum of Science and Industry which opened in 1983.

The two entrances on Liverpool Road led to the booking office. Having purchased a ticket, first class and second class passengers walked up separate staircases to the platform above. The Station Agent's House is next to the station, a brick building dating from the early 1800s.

Piccadilly Station

The Manchester-Birmingham line was completed in 1839, with the first London Road station opening in 1842 as the terminus of LNWR's trains from London. Its importance soon became obvious when the 24 hour coach journey to be capital was reduced to 12 hours by rail.

Through trains from Manchester to London were operated jointly by Manchester, Sheffield and Lincolnshire Railway (MSLR) and GNR in

24

Liverpool Road Passenger Station with the Station Agent's house on the left. Passengers entered via the two ground floor entrances, the more ornate one reserved for first class travellers.

A plaque reminding passers-by that Liverpool Road Station is a building of historic interest.

Located on the exterior wall of today's Piccadilly Station, the crest of the Manchester - Birmingham Railway carries the date 1839, the year when this route was completed.

The LNWR's London Road Station is at the top of a long approach.

Piccadilly Station approach today is flanked by the curving Gateway House.

1854. MSLR trains ran as far as Sheffield where GNR took them to King's Cross. The return fare from London-Manchester was five shillings (25 pence) in 1859. During 1866 the former Store Street Station was replaced by the Mills and Murgatroyd building which dominated the long station approach. Adjacent land was also used for constructing huge goods sheds and warehouses.

Because of increased traffic LNWR had to find alternative arrangements for London Road rail traffic and so in 1910 the nearby Mayfield Road Station was opened. It catered mainly for commuters from Manchester southern suburbs and it carried on as a parcels depot until the mid 1960s.

The electrification and modernisation of the Manchester-Crewe line brought considerable changes at London Road in 1959 and 1960. The Victorian offices and booking hall were removed, a new footbridge installed and in the early 1960s the concrete multi-storey building of Piccadilly Station's office block was opened. With its curved swoop of buildings, the approach is particularly impressive .

When the Sheffield line was electrified in mid 1950s EM2 Class Co-Co electric locomotives, later Class 77, were used. The London Road-Sheffield run took about one hour in the late 1950s.

Piccadilly Station is Manchester principal link with the south, its clean and functional appearance a far cry from Victorian days when it was covered in soot and grime. The journey to London now takes just over $2^1/_2$ hours and Piccadilly's future looks assured. Autumn 1988 brought disruptions for rail commuters at Piccadilly Station. It took engineers three weeks to renew 30-year-old signalling and lay new track as part of a £30m. scheme which incorporated the Windsor Link line. During the three week period Manchester's other main stations were temporarily closed.

Oxford Road Station

Established in 1849 the Manchester South Junction and Altrincham Railway had its terminus at Oxford Road until the 1890s. It took some of the pressure off London Road Station at a time when some 65 trains a day ran from Altrincham to Oxford Road. This encouraged the building of stations at Navigation Road and Dane Road catering for the increasing number of commuters from newly built houses.

Extensive alterations took place in 1959-1961 and the famous 'armadillo' shaped roof caused much controversy. Oxford Road Station goes into the 1990s with a £250,000 face lift and BR sees this as preparation for the station's more important rôle in Manchester rail network. The station building will be cleaned and a new car parking area will be provided in front of the station. Landscaping and general repairs to the perimeter wall should make life more pleasant for passengers, some of whom may take advantage of the new express services to the East Midlands and East Anglia.

Central Station

The G-Mex Centre is described elsewhere, but what about the structure when it served as a railway station?

A temporary station was in use from 1877 until 1880 when the permanent one was completed. Its impressive 210 feet roof span had its highest point 90 feet above the railway tracks. It was owned and used jointly by the Great Northern, Midland and Great Central Railway companies and as the terminus for the Cheshire Lines Committee whose trains ran between Manchester, Liverpool, Southport and into Cheshire.

Examples of popular routes from Central Station included the journey to Chinley via Tiviot Dale and Stockport. The famous Midland Pullman first came into service in 1960, leaving Central at 8.50 am, arriving in St. Pancras, London at 12.03 pm. There was only one stop at Cheadle Heath, Stockport and the first class single fare in 1960 was fifty seven shillings and sixpence.

Trains were gradually re-routed to Oxford Road and, in May 1969 Central Station closed, becoming a car park until it was renovated and rebuilt as G-Mex.

Victoria and Exchange Stations

Victoria Station opened on Hunt's Bank in 1844, and was concerned mainly with trains to the north, west and east of Manchester. The

Interior view at Piccadilly Station on a quiet Sunday morning.

Oxford Road Station's distinctive shaped 'armadillo' roof.

A train for Chester leaves Oxford Road Station.

The iron verandah outside Victoria Station still displays the names of places served by trains from Manchester.

LNWR had a route from Manchester to Leeds as far back as 1849 but owing to increased volume of rail traffic, it moved into its own station next to Victoria, Exchange Station, which derived its name from the nearby Cotton Exchange. The combined 2,194 foot Exchange-Victoria platform was the largest in Britain.

Local architect William Dawes designed Victoria's main building, housing the offices at the Lancashire and Yorkshire Railway. The principal routes of this company are shown on a large mural just inside the entrance hall. Victoria Station still has its impressive 160 foot long Edwardian front, displaying the names of places which the railway served.

Exchange Station closed down in 1969 and was later demolished. Today a car park occupies the site of this former railway station.

Knott Mill and Deansgate Station

Knott Mill and Deansgate Station was rebuilt in the late 19th century and its battlements are a reminder of the former Roman fort at Castlefield. The station is linked by bridge to the nearby G-Mex and today Deansgate caters for commuters who work in that area of the city. There are also regular services to places outside Manchester, of which the Liverpool line is quite popular.

British Rail in the 1990s

The summer of 1988 brought Super Sprinter trains to Manchester, the hub of a re-organised network of services linking the Fylde and Merseyside with South Yorkshire and East Anglia. As a consequence of this, passengers in Blackpool, for example, now have a direct link with Harwich, East Anglia.

Spring 1989 will see a de luxe version of the Sprinter introduced to the Manchester area. Using the new Windsor Link, opened in 1988, it brings together northern and southern services in the city between Ordsall Lane and Salford Crescent.

27

Manchester International Airport

A field in Burnage in April 1910 was the venue for the arrival of a flight from London by a Frenchman, Louis Paulham. This sparked off an interest in air travel in the north-west, which was then encouraged by the First World War through an important rôle in warfare. From 1911 to 1918 there was a privately owned aerodrome in Trafford Park.

A year later Alexandra Park, an ex-military airfield, was used for Avro Transport Company's service between Manchester, Southport and Blackpool. In 1922 Daimler Airway embarked on a Manchester-London service, which was extended to Berlin the following year. But then flying ceased at Alexandra Park in August 1924. Pressure forced Manchester Corporation to build an airport at Barton on Chat Moss near Manchester. In the meantime, a temporary airfield, Wythenshawe Airport, was established in a field at Rackhouse Farm, Northern Moor on 2nd April, 1929, the first municipal airport in Britain. Barton aerodrome came into operation in January 1930 in Chat Moss near Manchester.

Advancements in aircraft design meant that Barton's landing area could not cope. So, after KLM Royal Dutch Airlines had reviewed the possibility of a Manchester - Amsterdam service, in 1935 Manchester City Council received Air Ministry Approval for a new airport at Ringway, four miles south of the Wythenshawe temporary site. The original 600 acre Ringway airport was opened in 1938 just before the Second World War.

Many Manchester residents will remember Ringway's rôle in training paratroopers in the war when it came under the auspices of the RAF. In the transition from a civil airport to a military one the airport manager decided the large concrete letters spelling 'RINGWAY' from enemy 'planes. Local farmers were called in to help and they tipped huge loads of vegetables on the letters. In an effort to deter enemy landings the airport manager asked Manchester Corporation to send as many broken-down buses as possible. These were strategically placed as obstructions and give the impression that the airfield was a bus station.

Apart from the paratroopers, Ringway was also used to test and build

Victoria Station's façade bears the words 'Lancashire and Yorkshire Railway'.

Exchange Station (left) dates from 1884 and was approached by a bridge over the Irwell.

the prototype bombers made by A.V. Roe, including the famous Lancaster, Lincoln and Manchester bombers and Winston Churchill's own personal aircraft, the York transport plane 'Ascalon'. Many improvements were made to the airport during the war, including lengthening the runways.

Following the war, the Civil Aviation Act of 1946 encouraged the Ministry of Aviation to control Ringway but Manchester City Council opposed this. Not until 1953 was the fight finally won and the airport fully under the jurisdiction of local municipal authorities. Prior to the abolition of GMC, the running of Manchester Airport was in the hands of Manchester City Council and GMC. After the abolition of GMC and

following agreement between the ten Greater Manchester district councils, a public limited company was formed.

Today, along with New York, Paris and Zurich, Manchester is one of the world's top international airports. In 1979 the main runway was recontoured and extended in a mammoth series of night-time operations which took from March to November. During 1986 three new major intercontinental carriers were added to the list of airlines using the airport and the end of 1989 will see the completion of a new domestic facility accommodating much larger aircraft like Tri-Stars and DC-10s. Some 51 airlines now fly to over 130 destinations from Manchester to every European centre, the USA, Canada, the Middle and Far East, Australia and India.

Britain's first Airborne Forces trained in large numbers at Ringway Airport during the Second World War. Converted Whitley bombers were used for early parachute training.

August 10th, 1959 at Manchester's airport. The huts in the foreground were soon to be replaced by the building under construction at the rear. It is hard to imagine that this was the scene just 30 years ago!

The new Air Terminus for Manchester in Cross Street, 1952.

Manchester International Airport to-day.

It is 1896 and the steam tug 'Stretford' hauls four loaded barges (off picture) on the Rochdale Canal.

Workers reconstruct Piccadilly Lock on the Rochdale Canal, 1880.

5. Waterways

For some people Manchester's waterways are a thing of the past, their history hidden in the murky waters which meander under buildings and bridges in the city. However, it should be stressed that canals and rivers in the area have played a major rôle in Manchester's development, a city standing at the confluence of the Rivers Irk, Medlock and Irwell. The soft water from rivers and streams made a vital contribution to Manchester's cotton industry. The Ship Canal and Docks were opened in 1894 and the city became a principal port, while other canals encouraged expansion of commerce and industry.

The Canals

The Rochdale Canal

Dating from 1804, this canal was the most important waterway link between Lancashire and Yorkshire. It was augmented in 1811 by the Huddersfield Narrow Canal and in 1818 by the Leeds-Liverpool Canal. The Rochdale Canal is some 33 miles in length, has 92 locks and runs between the Hebble Navigation (Sowerby Bridge) and Castlefield, Manchester, where it joins the Bridgewater Canal.

The locks on the Rochdale Canal could accommodate craft 74 feet by 14 feet 2 inches. Cargo in the early 1800s included stone, lime, coal, corn, timber, salt and wool. The Rochdale Canal Company offered an impressive Express Service until the First World War, transporting goods along the 33 miles in an incredible 36 hours. In 1937 the last loaded barge travelled the complete length of the canal from Manchester to Sowerby Bridge. Some coal traffic operated on the Manchester section until the early 1950s.

In 1952 the Rochdale Canal Act took away the legal obligation of the Rochdale Canal Company to maintain the waterway for through navigation. Only 1¼ miles of the canal in Manchester's centre was kept open for navigation mainly because it formed part of the busy Cheshire Ring.

In the early and mid-1980s work was carried out between Todmorden and Hebden Bridge. The Rochdale Canal Trust was formed by Calderdale and West Yorkshire councils and the Canal Company to look after the restored length of the waterway in West Yorkshire.

So what does the Manchester stretch look like today? By 1972 two sections of the canal between Stotts Lane and Hulme Hall Lane, Varley Street and Murray Street had been developed as a linear park by the City Council. Extensive areas of the canalside have been landscaped while locks 74, 78, 79 and 81 have been removed and others cascaded.

A section of the canal within the vicinity of Great Ancoats Street was landscaped and fully restored during 1983, including the removal of Lock 82. Beyond Dale Street the stretch of the canal is referred to as the 'Rochdale Nine' and its navigable waterway is a valuable link on the Cheshire Ring between the Bridgewater and Ashton Canals. Recent environmental improvement work has enhanced the stretch between Deansgate and the Railway Viaduct, and the lock-keeper's cottage at lock 92 has been renovated. It is in the Castlefield area that the canal cuts through red sandstone and joins the Bridgewater Canal.

The Bridgewater Canal

Work on the Bridgewater Canal commenced in 1759 under the direction of two engineers John Gilbert and James Brindley. It was designed to bring coal from the Duke of Bridgewater's mines at Worsley to Manchester. Partially opened in 1761, this canal was independent of any existing river or waterway, thus marking quite a departure from normal canal construction. A coal wharf was built in Castlefield, soon followed by a large basin and several warehouses below today's Castle Street.

The Bridgewater Canal had a pronounced effect on Manchester when businessmen realised that in addition to coal, items like timber, cotton, grain and salt could be readily transported. This, of course, encouraged the development of Knott Mill and Castlefield which became warehouse centres for such commodities as corn, timber, flour, cereal and potatoes (see the 'Oxnoble' pub in the Chapter on Wining and Dining).

The 'Shamrock' has been forced to a halt by thick ice on the Rochdale Canal in the winter of 1888.

Pictured in 1919 at Dale Street Wharf, Manchester, this motor lorry was later requisitioned for army use in France during the First World War.

The restored lock-keeper's cottage at Lock 92 on the Rochdale Canal.

A view of the Bridgewater Canal where it passes under a railway viaduct which carried rail traffic to Central Station.

Sadly, time took its toll on the area and the Castlefield section of the Bridgewater Canal looked in a poor state during the 1960s. However, in 1979 Castlefield was designated a Conservation Area by the City Council and the 1980s brought about the restoration of basins on the Bridgewater and Rochdale Canals. During 1988 a major scheme has begun on renovating the Bridgewater towpath in the city centre, creating a public waterway from the city boundary into the heart of the city. This £125,000 scheme has also opened up the only section of the towpath on the Cheshire Ring which remained inaccessible to the public. A 1¼ mile stretch between the Cornbrook Bridge at Old Trafford and Merchant's Warehouse near Deansgate has been restored and transformed in time for the August 1988 National Boat Rally.

For those wishing to explore part of the canal, why not take advantage of the packet boat service which operates on Sundays from the Duke of Bridgewater's former home in Worsley and from the Castlefield Basin?

The Ashton Canal

Linking Manchester with Ashton, this canal's construction was permitted by an Act of Parliament in 1792. The route was designed to take it along the south side of the River Medlock and a further Act of 1793 allowed the owners to run a branch towards Stockport and to build a link to Hollinwood. This would enable coal to be carried from pits in places like Haughton Green and Werneth.

The end of 1796 witnessed the completion of the canal between Ancoats in Manchester and Ashton, and the Stockport link opened a year later. The Ashton Canal Company ordered warehouses to be built at Piccadilly in 1798 on Lord Ducie's land and the following year saw the completion of a branch to Piccadilly.

After a number of differences with the Rochdale Canal Company the junction with the Ashton and Rochdale Canals at Piccadilly was finally opened. The Piccadilly-Ashton link was 6¾ miles in length, the main section rising from Manchester by means of 18 locks and aqueducts in four places, including Ancoats and Beswick. The Ashton Canal carried

33

a variety of commodities and provided a passenger service from Piccadilly to Ashton, leaving Manchester at 8.00 am and departing from Ashton at 4.00 p.m. In 1848, the waterway was purchased by the Manchester, Sheffield and Lincolnshire Railway (which later became the Great Central). This company also assumed ownership of the Peak Forest and Macclesfield Canals and it provided facilities for links at Ashton and London Road, Manchester. Things worked out well until 1892 when the railway company ceased to use the canals to carry their goods and dissolved the canal companies.

Competition from road transport has always affected canals and the Ashton Canal was no exception as pre-Second World War years led to a dramatic fall in tonnage carried by vessels.

Following the war little maintenance was carried out and there followed a general state of disrepair with several blockages appearing by 1960. However, mainly to the efforts of local enthusiasts the towpaths and locks had been cleared of rubbish. The relentless work by these volunteers has ensured the reopening of the Ashton Canal. Walkers can pick up the towpath off Ducie Street just past Jutland Street in the vicinity of the Ashton Canal Basin. Early 1989 will see the start of a five-acre waterside village complex in this area of Manchester. The hub of the project will be the Ashton Canal which is to have a new bridge. Furthermore a new canal basin is to be built between the Ashton Canal and Chapeltown Street.

The Manchester Ship Canal

This marvellous feat of engineering is 36 miles long, connecting Eastham Locks on the River Mersey with Manchester. Work began in 1885 when the whole of the route was divided into nine sections with an engineer in charge of each. The first one stretched from Eastham's tidal entrance to Ellesmere Port while the last section was from Barton to Manchester. This ninth part of the route included several locks and swing bridges such as the aqueduct at Barton where the Ship Canal cut across the route of the Bridgewater Canal. The construction of the 'inland seaway' presented engineers with numerous challenges. The estuary outside Eastham docks had to be dredged, granite from

34

Bustling Manchester Docks in 1969.

The approach (right) to the Ashton Canal Basin, Manchester.

Cornwall was shipped in to build locks, and the road and rail crossings are a tribute to the skill of the engineers.

Flooding in 1890 damaged locks at Eastham and the elements often plagued the Ship Canal's construction. In 1892, for instance, cold weather held up concreting, and in the same year a particularly large tide rushed up the Mersey and damaged the Bridgewater Lock.

In spite of all these problems, the canal was dug and agreements were made with railway companies where lines had to be lifted above the waterway. The average number of navigators or 'navvies' employed was 12,000 and they moved nearly 70 million tons of earth and rock. Accidents were commonplace, with 1,300 taking place in the five years leading to 1892. Eventually, the scheme was completed and in November 1893 the last section began to be filled with water.

In December, the Company directors travelled the full length of the canal in a steamship. On January 1st, 1894, traffic was allowed on the waters and Queen Victoria officiated at the formal opening of the canal in May of that year. Manchester had now been linked to the sea.

The amount of shipping declined in the 1980s, although a few vessels still ply as far as the Irwell Lock. The annual Manchester Ship Canal Cruise took to the waters again in 1988 as a record number of Mancunians took advantage of the 36-mile trip. For £12 a head, they obtained a close-up of exciting new developments taking place around the Ship Canal-Salford Quays, the Barton aqueduct, and the Trafford Park Development. The $6^1/_2$ hour journey has been running every year since 1945. In 1988, the historic swing-bridge at Trafford was re-housed. Straddling the Manchester Ship Canal for 40 years, the 550-ton bridge was floated to its new home. Following a clean-up, the bridge became a decorative feature of Salford Quays as well as acting as a link-up between docks for sightseers and for owners of prestigious new homes developed nearby.

Other Canals

The Manchester, Bolton and Bury Canal

This canal was intended as a waterway link between Bolton and Bury and the River Irwell. Encouraged by an Act of 1791 it was finally opened in 1808. Raised by six locks from the Irwell to the basin at Oldfield Road, Salford, the canal continued along the Irwell Valley to Bolton. Eleven miles in length, it had a $4^3/_4$ mile branch built to Bury. Examples of commodities carried included coal and limestone.

The Company's Act of 1831 gave the owners a rather lengthy title - the Company of Proprietors of the Manchester, Bolton and Bury Canal Navigation and Railway. This organisation was granted power to construct a line from Manchester to Bolton and Bury, closely following the canal's route. The first passengers were carried in 1838 but the railway did not attract as much freight from road transport as had been hoped and in 1848 the Company amalgamated with the Manchester and Leeds Railway.

The waterway to Bolton and Bury proved its worth until the Second World War when a $1/_2$ mile section at Clifton Junction was drained as a measure against flooding in the event of enemy bombing raids. Acts of 1941 and 1961 did nothing to promote the canal's future and it was abandoned in several sections and fell into disrepair. In spite of the decline in the canal, 1989 may see enthusiasts talking of a major restoration project, although much of the stretch through Salford has been filled in.

The Manchester and Salford Junction Canal

Connecting the Rochdale Canal to the River Irwell at Water Street, this waterway of just over half a mile long dates from 1839. The last commercial traffic was carried in the 1920s. Many observers considered it to be a white elephant as high running costs and technical problems overshadowed its opening. The advent of the railways created many problems for canals including the Manchester and Salford Junction. The Cheshire Lines Committee Railway decided to build their Central Station over the canal in 1872 with an Act of 1875 bringing about the closure of the canal between Lower Mosley Street and Watson Street where it was filled in.

Today a section of the 180-year-old canal now forms part of the new underpass access route to G-Mex's underground car parks. There is

Two large vessels pass each other on the Ship Canal at Cadishead, 1953 with a tug fore   and aft. The ship on the left is an unladen tanker, the vessel on the right is bound for Manchester, laden with timber.

The River Irwell forms a convenient boundary between Manchester and Salford. The Victoria Bridge (foreground) dates from 1839 and features two orbs on inscribed scrolls.

still a portion of the original waterway remaining under the Centre, but it is accessed down a long inspection chamber.

The Rivers

Manchester is situated on the east bank of the River Irwell where it joins the Irk and Medlock. The Roman camp at Castlefield was built on a sandstone crag in a loop of the River Medlock near the confluence with the two other rivers, and it is likely the Romans had a ford across the Medlock. This was superseded by a bridge where today the river flows under Deansgate. The Medlock, of course, was once the boundary between the townships of Hulme and Manchester.

Towards the end of the 18th century much of Manchester was contained between the Rivers Irk, Irwell and Medlock. This was a poor run-down area where disease and sickness were rampant, since the squalid buildings lacked proper drainage or sanitary provision. The River Irwell formed the boundary between Manchester and Salford and was traversed by the Blackfriars Bridge (1761) and the Victoria Bridge (1839) which replaced the old Salford Bridge.

The Irwell played its part in the cotton industry with many mills springing up along its banks in the 1800s. The firm Mather and Platt began its life in 1846 as an ironworks adjacent to the Irwell and one of its early products was a steamship which sailed down the Irwell, along the Mersey and then on to the Isle of Man.

6. *Leisure and Pleasure*

Greater Manchester has everything one would expect of an area with nearly three million inhabitants. The city's museums, theatres, galleries and specialist libraries receive high acclaim from around the world. Lovers of all types of music are catered for from pop to opera in Manchester. The cosmopolitan nature of the city is reflected in its variety of eating and drinking establishments to suit all tastes. The media is well represented here, while United and City Football Clubs, and Lancashire Cricket Club are internationally famous.

These many aspects of recreation are not new to Manchester - Kersal Moor used to be the venue for Manchester Races, and Manchester Wheelers catering for those interested in cycling was founded in 1883. Belle Vue Zoological Gardens opened its doors in 1836 and, of course, Manchester's many parks are an integral part of community life. Queen's Park and Philips Park came into existence in the mid-1860s. Whitworth Park dates from 1890, taking its name from Sir Joseph Whitworth and providing almost 19 acres of greenery, flower beds and a lake.

Sport

Manchester United

When referring to Manchester abroad it is more than likely to provoke the rejoinder - 'Manchester United'. There is no doubt that the glamorous club is just as popular today as when it won the European Cup in 1968. So how did it all start?

The precise date of inauguration is not known, since the club did not appear on historical records until 1878 when it was called Newton Heath. The team entered the First Division in 1892 as Manchester City moved into Division Two. Wearing a strip of green and gold, Newton Heath lost their first match to Blackburn, 3-4. Later relegated to Division Two, the renamed Manchester United battled to regain Division One status and were promoted with Bristol City in 1906.

Modern amenities have provided better recreational facilities than this inner city waste ground in the 1950s.

Manchester United FC, 1913-14. No honours for the club this season when Blackburn Rovers were top of Division One, while Burnley and Liverpool reached the FA Cup Final.
Back row (l to r) Hodge, Gripps, Knowles, Beale, Stacey, Hamill, Whalley
Front row (l to r) Meredith, Woodcock, Anderson, West, Wall

Some famous players in the early 1900s included Sandy Turnbull, George Wall, Billy Meredith and, of course, Captain Charlie Roberts. United moved to the Old Trafford ground in 1910 and were relegated to Division Two in 1922. Two years later they fought back and re-entered Division One, going down again in 1931. Times were hard. Players were not paid in 1931 because the bank would not extend a large overdraft. The team battled desperately to regain First Division Status, moving up in 1936 but going down again the following season.

Supporters must have been exasperated by United's yo-yo movement between Divisions, although the club gained promotion by finishing runners-up to Aston Villa in 1938. During the Second World War, Old Trafford was badly damaged by bombs. At that time 35-year-old Matt Busby was appointed manager. Soon afterwards Jimmy Murphy was made his assistant .

Players in post-war teams included John Aston, Henry Cockburn, Stan Pearson and Eddie Quigley. The forward line was a formidable force whose superb attacking moves came from such people as Delaney, Pearson, Mitten, Rowley and Morris.

United won the FA Cup in 1948. The early 1950s brought full houses to Old Trafford when Bill Foulkes, Ray Wood, Tommy Taylor, Roger Byrne and Duncan Edwards entertained the supporters. This was the era of the 'Busby Babes' and in 1955 United reached the 4th round of the FA Cup but were knocked out by Manchester City.

The Munich tragedy of 1958 shook the world and some observers felt the club would not recover. But United were determined to regain their former glory, signing Albert Quixall from Sheffield Wednesday in 1960/61 at a time when Noel Cantwell, Tony Dunne, David Herd and Nobby Stiles joined the squad.

In 1963 Dennis Law became an expensive buy at a record £115,000, from Torino, Italy - the club to which he had gone after leaving Manchester City. George Best first played for United in 1964 against West Bromwich and two years later the club finished 4th in Division One, reaching the FA Cup Semi-Final for their fifth successive year. 1968 brought success for United as the first English Club to win the European Cup with a superb 4-1 victory over Benfica.

In the 1970s Frank O'Farrell was appointed Manager with Sir Matt Busby joining the Board in 1972. 1974 meant relegation for the first time since 1937 but in true United fashion the club was back in Division One in 1975. Their Wembley triumph of 1978 saw them beat Liverpool 2-1 in the FA Cup Final and in the closed season Dave Sexton succeeded Tommy Docherty as manager.

United paid and received new club record transfer fees in the 1978/80 season. Ray Wilkins was signed from Chelsea for £825,000 and Brian Greenhoff went to Leeds for £350,000.

Ron Atkinson took over the manager's job in 1981. 1983 was one of the club's most successful seasons ever. Finishing third in Division One, United beat Everton in the FA cup. Jesper Olsen and Gordon Strachan joined the squad in the mid-1980s, a time when ground improvements included the link of the cantilever stand. This provided the ground with unrestricted viewing facilities encompassing three quarters of the stadium.

In 1986, United finished fourth in Division One and Mark Hughes left for Barcelona. In this year the Museum and Visitor's Centre was unveiled. During the following season, manager Ron Atkinson departed, to be replaced by Alex Ferguson. Rugby League came to Old Trafford during 1987 when Great Britain played Australia in October, with the Premiership Finals taking place in May. In the 1988 season United finished second behind Division One leaders Liverpool and the soccer 'A' team won the Lancashire League, Division One. United's 'B' team were runners-up in the Lancashire League, Division Two.

Manchester City

The club was formed in 1880 as West Gorton St Marks, changing its name to Ardwick FC when it moved to Hyde Road during 1887. The team played in the Football Alliance, which became Division Two of the Football League in 1892, in the year in which Ardwick finished fifth in their first season. The 1898/99 season took the newly named Manchester City into Division One, and in 1904 City beat Bolton Wanderers to win the FA Cup and also finished runners-up in the League Championship.

City's first Continental tour took place in 1910 and they moved to Maine Road in 1923 where they won their first game against Sheffield, 2-1. In that year Billy Meredith was given a free transfer from Manchester United and joined City, where he played for a further season. 1926 brought its ups and downs, with City becoming FA Cup Finalists, losing 1-0 to Bolton in the Final. Unfortunately, City were relegated, missing promotion in 1927 and Portsmouth was promoted instead.

The club persevered, reaching the Cup Final in 1933 and becoming the FA Cup Winners of 1934 when it defeated Portsmouth 2-1. They won the First Division Championship for the first time in 1937 but were relegated in 1938, despite scoring 80 goals - more than any other First Division club! Neighbours Manchester United had also joined the Second Division in 1937.

The post-war years witnessed City gain promotion to Division One in 1947 and fighting off advances by United, who tried to buy their goalkeeper Frank Swift.

City supporters could enjoy evening games in 1953 with the installation of floodlights and two years later the club reached the FA Cup Final for the first time in 21 years. Older supporters will remember this game. City lost 1-0 to Newcastle United, their defeat partly attributable to playing with only 10 men following the injury to full-back Jimmy Meadows.

The 1956 FA Cup Final was also hit by injury when City defeated Birmingham City 3-1, despite goalkeeper Bert Trautmann playing much of the second half with a broken neck!

The club dropped back to Division Two in 1963 but the combination of Joe Mercer and Malcolm Allison took them to Division One in 1966. Two years later they became First Division Champions for the second time and in 1969 City were FA Cup Winners, beating Leicester City 1-0.

The club acquired a unique double in 1970, beating West Bromwich to win the Football League Cup and later defeating Poland's Gornik Zabrze to win the European Cup Winner's Cup.

The City first team in the mid-1940s.

Maine Road action as City try for a goal in 1988.

The cricket ground at Old Trafford.

A view of Granada TV's office block in May 1961, just after its construction at a cost of £500,000. Note the interesting selection of cars and the absence of to-day's ubiquitous parking meters.

Newcastle were beaten 2-1 by City in the 1970 League Cup Final at Wembley and the Manchester Club finished runners-up in Division One the following season. Unfortunately, 1983 meant relegation to Division Two where City remained for two years until Billy McNeill and Jimmy Frizzell took the club into Division One. 1987 discovered City moving down once more to the Second Division where they finished ninth in 1988.

Lancashire County Cricket Club

The LCC is found in Old Trafford quite close to Manchester United's ground. Although both clubs are located in Trafford Metropolitan Borough, they are usually associated with Manchester. This is hardly surprising since the game of cricket flourished in Manchester during the early 1800s when there was a club whose ground was in the Hulme district.

Examples of early recorded games played by the Manchester Cricket Club include one against a military team, while in 1842 they sent a team to Lords to play the MCC. The club later moved to Chester Road, occupying the site of the White City Greyhound Stadium. Eventually, the title Lancashire County and Manchester Cricket Club evolved and the club relocated to the present Old Trafford ground in 1857.

It was decided that a County Club would best serve the interests of the game west of the Pennines, and following a meeting at the Queen's Hotel, Manchester in 1864, a County Cricket Club was formed.

Gradually, the fixture list built up and Lancashire became County Championship Winners in 1879, 1881, 1882, 1889, 1897 and 1904.

During the First World War the pavilion at Old Trafford was employed as a hospital for injured servicemen. Players of the 1920s included McDonald, Tyldesley, Sibbles, Parkin and Duckworth whose efforts led to the club becoming Championship winners in 1926, 1927, 1928, 1930 and 1934. Payner hit an historic century against Yorkshire during the mid-1930s at a time when Sibbles was the team's principal bowler.

During the Second World War Old Trafford acted as an army depot for the Royal Engineers. The next main trophy came in 1950 when

41

once again the Championship Winner's award was won. Examples of famous players since then have included Dyson, Statham, Lloyd, Bond, Pilling, Lever, Engineer, Haghurst, Fowler and Fairbrother.

The 1988 season opened with a championship game against Worcestershire and a new £40,000 pitch cover was introduced at the ground. Protecting an area of 200 feet by 100 feet, it stands 14 feet fully inflated and has helped to save many games from the elements.

Television and Radio

Manchester has much to offer in terms of television and radio stations. It is served by a number of companies including Radio Piccadilly which celebrated its tenth anniversary in 1988.

Granada Television

On May 3rd, 1956, Granada Television went on the air. On this opening night viewers saw 'Meet the People' and 'Tribute to the BBC'. Royal Assent was given to the Television Bill in 1954 and Granada Television Limited was formed in February 1955 with work commencing on Granada Television Centre in August of the same year. Studio 2 was the first custom-built studio designed specifically for television.

So who would see Granada TV? Well, it served the whole of the North of England, coast-to-coast, from Lancashire to Yorkshire until 1968 when Yorkshire Television was created to serve the eastern region from Leeds. The programmes in the 1950s and 1960s heralded the way for Granada's varied and stimulating transmissions which are still with us. Do you remember Manchester United -v- Real Madrid on April 25th, 1957? It was watched by people in 1,000,000 homes. The programme 'Criss Cross Quiz' of 1958 saw £2,360 awarded as the highest prize ever, and 'Coronation Street' made its first appearance on December 9th, 1960. Examples of other programmes which came into living rooms were 'University Challenge' in 1962 and 'World in Action' in 1963.

During 1969 the present Granada logo made its début and this year brought the first colour transmissions. Building took place in the 1960s with studios 8 and 12 constructed in 1962, while the TV centre office block was completed the previous year. 1973 brought the opening of studio 8 and six years later a £6m. re-equipment scheme was begun at the TV Centre.

During 1980, IBA renewed Granada's contract until 1990 and in 1983 Bamber Gascoigne completed 21 non-stop years of University Challenge. The following year was 'World in Action's' 21st anniversary and in 1985 five British Academy Awards were given for 'The Jewel in the Crown'.

Recent years have witnessed an authentic reconstruction of the House of Commons in Stage One for Jeffrey Archer's 'First Among Equals' in 1986. In the same year the Government extended ITV contracts to 1992.

During 1987 work started on £8m. Granada Studios Tour project allowing visitors to have a $3\frac{1}{4}$ hour trip behind-the-scenes of TV and film production. That year also meant that Bamber Gascoigne and University Challenge shared the 25th anniversary of Britain's longest-running TV quiz.

Leading the way

Granada has always been at the forefront of new advances and technological expertise. In drama, the company is renowned as the most adventurous of British programme makers, typified by 'The Jewel in the Crown' which followed the highly acclaimed 'Brideshead Revisited'. Len Deighton's trilogy of spy novels 'Game, Set and Match' appear on the ITV network in 1988, while the weekly 'World in Action' has won more than 55 British and International awards for TV journalism since its first appearance in 1963.

The Company Today

Granada serves some $6\frac{1}{2}$ million viewers in an area from just south of the Lake District to North Staffordshire, the Dee Estuary and the North Wales coast to the Pennines. Visit the TV Centre in Manchester and

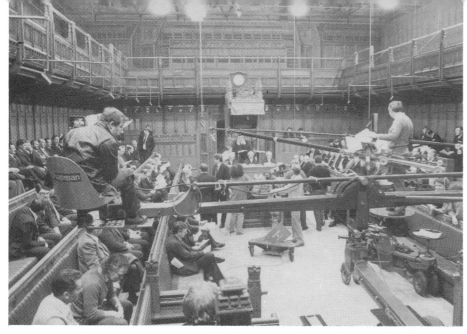

An authentic reconstruction of the chamber of the House of Commons for Jeffrey Archer's 'First Among Equals'.

Granada's new Ikegami cameras in action at Studio 12 in the Manchester Television Centre, 1987.

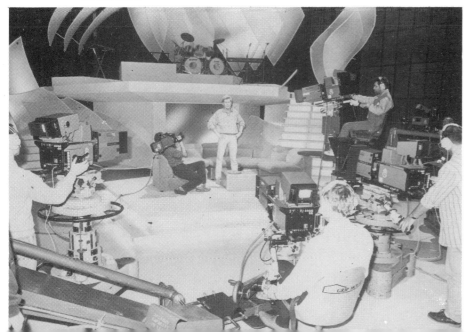

you will discover an impressive 15 acre site comprising four principal studios. The 14,000 square foot floor-space production Building-Stage One, provides further video and film facilities next to Baker Street and Coronation Street outdoor location sets.

Granada has Britain's most modern electronic Newsroom in the converted office of Liverpool's reconstructed Albert Dock complex. This set-up can receive and transmit national and international news by means of satellite and is the nerve centre for Granada's news operation.

Why 'Granada'?
Lord Bernstein is the Group's President and the name was his choice. During the 1920s he arrived in the City of Granada in Spain, fell in love with its charm and beauty, and decided to use the name for his string of theatres. For all subsequent developments - TV, Motorways, TV Rental and Publishing - this was the name he adopted. It seems to be a very lucky name too!

The BBC

Broadcasts began in the north of England in 1922 from a room in Old Trafford. Seven years later the BBC moved to Broadcasting House, Piccadilly and this centre soon developed a reputation from current affairs, comedy and sports commentary. It was also the base for the Northern Dance Orchestra under the baton of Sir Charles Groves.

Television appeared in the north in 1951 when a former Wesleyan Church in Dickenson Road, Longsight became the first TV studio to be brought into operation outside London. It was the home for a number of long-running programmes, including 'Top of the Pops'. BBC's move to its present location in Oxford Road, Manchester occurred in 1975. A large studio complex housed television studios, a radio drama suite and a television news operation. The local news magazine programme 'North West Tonight' is presented on weekdays by a number of personalities, including Stuart Hall and John Munday. Oxford Road is also the base for BBC Radio Manchester and it provides a concert hall for the BBC Philharmonic Orchestra.

43

'North West Tonight' presenters Stuart Hall and John Munday.

The BBC in the north-west has a long tradition of making radio programmes, dating to the early days of the crystal set. Today it supplies 1300 hours of radio each year to four national networks - Radios 1,2, 3 and 4.

Many of the TV programmes made in the north west are seen in several regions of the country, and some 350 programmes are currently made for BBC 1 and BBC 2.

Examples of well known TV programmes from BBC North West include 'Brass Tacks', 'Open Air', 'It's a Knockout', 'A Question of Sport' plus several programmes for children.

The award winning 'File on 4' is the radio news and current affairs flagship from the north-west. 'Gardeners' Question Time' celebrated its 40th anniversary in 1987 and is set to carry on well into the 21st century. This programme from the north-west has provided answers for more than 17,000 questions over the years.

BBC Radio and Television operations in the north-west reflect the cultural, commercial and sporting interests of the region in addition to producing programmes for the national networks.

7. Wining and Dining

"Dis-moi ce que tu manges, je te dirai ce que tu es", said Brillat-Savarin: "Tell me what you eat, I'll tell you what you are."

The range of restaurants in Manchester specialise in cuisines from all corners of the globe and there is no doubt that the choice of restaurant can often give a clue as to the character of the person involved.

Nearly thirty of Manchester's restaurants feature in the *'Good Food Guide'* and it is possible to try a different national dish every night for a month! There are, of course, well know establishments catering for the discerning drinker and diner with the 'Sawyer's Arms' and 'Mr Thomas's Chop House' being two examples. Situated on Deansgate the 'Sawyer's' has a fine example of a typical Victorian pub façade, while Mr. Thomas's on Cross Street demonstrates a form of Edwardian architecture. A busy lunch time pub with a fine selection of food, Mr. Thomas's serves hand-pumped Thwaites bitter and mild, plus Chester's bitter.

To appreciate fully the range of food available in Manchester and its suburbs how about perusing this list. One famous eating establishment is then considered in some detail - the 'Yang Sing'.

Food	Name	Location
American	Great Chicago Diner	Wilmslow Rd, Withington
Bangladeshi	Evert	Whitworth Street
Chinese	Mai Wah	Barlow Moor Road
	Yang Sing	Princess Street
Danish	Herriot's Danish Centre	Cross Street
Dutch	Dutch Pancake House	St.Peters's Sq
English	Barnaby Rudge	Old Bank Street
	Sam's Chop House	Chapel Walks
	City Limits	Burnage
French	Truffles	Bridge Street
	L'Auberge de France	Platt Lane
Greek	Acropolis Taverna	Princess Street
	Five Kings	Chester Road
Indian	Bengal	Chapel Street
	Star of India	Oxford Road
Italian	Cesare Ristorante Italiano	South King Street
Japanese	Mina - Japan	George Street
Korean	Amigos	Deansgate
Nepalese	Kathmandu	Sackville Street
Persian	Khyam	Richmond Street
Spanish	Casa Espana	Wilmslow Road
Thai	Siam Orchid Thai	Portland Street
Turkish	Café Istanbul	Bridge Street

It is interesting to note that ethnic restaurants tend to be found near each other. In Rusholme, for example, one finds a plethora of Indian eating places which are popular with students and permanent residents alike. Wilmslow Road, Rusholme is the home of the Al-Noor Restaurant, the Ambala Sweet centre, Paradise Restaurant and the Saman Sweet Centre. The gourmet can also enjoy the Polash Tandoori and The Tandoori Kitchen which are found in this stretch of Wilmslow Road.

Other restaurants include vegetarian establishments like 'That Café' in Levenshulme plus 'On the Eighth Day' restaurant on Oxford Road.

The Yang Sing Restaurant

Mention the Yang Sing restaurant, Manchester and people will immediately think of superlatives such as 'the best in Europe', 'the best anywhere outside Hong Kong'. Naturally, this renowned eating place has featured in the *'Good Food Guide'* and it is known at home and abroad as one of the leading Cantonese restaurants. So, why this fame and popularity?

No doubt its location in a flourishing Chinese business community has helped trade. Chinese people from all over the north-west visit the

啟者：花城酒樓三月
六日啟市營業
晚飯茶式小菜供應
暫因改裝點心炸燴
由四月三日起精美點心
全日供應 請原諒

RESTAURANT
OPEN

SPECIAL
4 COURSE
LUNCH
£2·60
EXECUTIVE LUNCH
£5·50
FROM 12 TO 2 P.m

46 This bi-lingual notice appears outside a Chinese Restaurant in Manchester's centre.

The impressive Victorian façade of the Yang Sing Restaurant, Princess Street.

area bounded by Mosley Street and Portland Street to carry out business transactions and to do more mundane things like visiting the dentist or hairdresser. Where better to round off a busy day than in the Yang Sing?

The Yang Sing moved from its original tiny premises in George Street to the present Princess Street location in 1984-85. The exterior of the restaurant at 34 Princess Street features Victorian architecture and has five storeys. Within the building one discovers Conference Suites and a Boardroom which are used by many companies for one-day conferences and seminars as well as corporate entertainment. Of course, any restaurant with as many media awards as the Yang Sing will attract numerous customers. Early reservations are essential and it has been known for staff to take bookings from such places as Basle, Hong Kong and Hobart.

Needless to say the cuisine is first class. The range is terrific with about 350 different items on the à la carte menu alone. The Author would recommend fillet steak, Cantonese style.

Since moving to Princess Street, the old premises on George Street have re-opened in early 1988 as the Little Yang Sing, providing the same excellent quality of food as its larger brother.

Public Houses

Seen by many as the Mecca for serious beer drinkers, Manchester provides a wide range of real ales. Local independent brewers include Hyde's, Holt, Lees, Boddington's and Robinson's in nearby Stockport. Examples of other independents with outlets in Manchester are Burtonwood, Thwaites, Samuel Smith's, Banks's and Marston's. Beer is also on sale from such companies as Bass, Tetley and Greenall.

Clearly, it is not possible to provide a complete compendium of all pubs in Manchester. Some famous city centre pubs will be looked at and also some less well known places in the suburbs. It should be noted that pubs change hands and landlords may bring in new types of beer. The information in this section was correct at the time of writing.

The City Centre

Manchester's centre provides a good cross-section of interesting pubs, many of which sell real ale. Before looking at some of these, one ought to refer to a hostelry called the 'Seven Stars Inn'. It stood on Shudehill and claimed to be the oldest licensed premises in Great Britain and that its first licence was granted in 1358 during the reign of Edward III. However, it must be stated that the first reference to a licence in connection with a public house dates from 1551 and prior to that anyone could sell ale. Legends suggest that the 'Seven Stars' was visited by Guy Fawkes and Bonnie Prince Charlie. The building was demolished in 1911.

Today's lover of good beer and interesting surroundings could do worse than to try some of these city centre pubs. The 'Circus Tavern' on Portland Street has Tetley Walker mild and Tetley bitter, while the 'Harp and Shamrock', New Mount Street, provides Marston's beers. The 'City Arms' on Kennedy Street is a Tetley Walker house and John Smiths products are available at the nearby 'Vine', which was refurbished in 1988. The 'Rising Sun' is a haven for drinkers who like a pub off the beaten track and 'Tommy Ducks' is handy for G-Mex and local office workers. When visiting this last place (named after one of its landlords, Tommy Duckworth) have a look at the ceiling which is festooned with articles of ladies' underwear!

If your journey takes you out of Piccadilly towards the south, keep an eye open for the 'Brunswick' on the left just before the Piccadilly Station approach. This busy pub features doorways with Doric columns and is a favourite haunt of commuters who have half an hour to spare before catching their train.

The Wellington Inn

It is said that this building dates from the early 14th century, but it is more likely to have been constructed around 1550. Subsequent rebuilding has altered its appearance quite dramatically. A private house until becoming a pub in 1830, it is famous as the birthplace of

48   When visiting 'Tommy Ducks' have a glance at the garments pinned to the ceiling!

Handy for a quick lunch time pint, the 'Rising Sun' hides among tall office buildings.

The 'Seven Stars' inn - reputedly the oldest licensed premises in Britain - was located on Shudehill. It was demolished in 1911.

An interesting view of the 'Wellington Inn' on Old Shambles Market Place in October 1900. During the Second World War much of the adjacent property was destroyed by a German land mine.

the author John Byrom, best remembered as the writer of *'Christians Awake'* and as the inventor of a phonetic shorthand.

The 'Wellington' can claim to be the sole example of an old timber-framed building in the City Centre and it originally stood in one of the places where Manchester's commerce began, the Market Place. During the Second World War a German land mine destroyed much of the older property in its vicinity.

Some Manchester residents will remember the summer of 1971 when the whole building was raised 4 feet 9½ inches on a concrete raft during the Market Street redevelopment scheme before being raised further off the ground to its present position in Shambles Square.

Sinclair's

'Sinclair's', next to the old 'Wellington Inn', was also raised during redevelopment in 1971. It is probable that a building has stood here since the 1300s. Sinclair's is located on the site of the first John Shaw Punch House, started by Mr. Shaw in 1738. Its position in the bustling Smithy Door district encouraged a steady trade in punch. The Punch House was the venue for Manchester's first gentlemen's club and around 1845 oysters were introduced to the premises, with further alcoholic beverages following in 1865. Fifteen square yards of the site of the old Punch house is now occupied by the north-west corner of Sinclair's.

The Castle and Falcon

Hiding in Bradshaw Street in Manchester's Shudehill area, this hostelry was an ancient lock-up for criminals. In fact, one miscreant was taken from the premises and hanged in 1783. Located in the heart of Manchester's newspaper world, the 'Castle and Falcon' is a popular meeting place for journalists. Bar snacks and cask-conditioned Burtonwood ales are on sale in this pub.

49

Today's 'Wellington' still has traces of its past.

'Sinclair's' stands on the site of John Shaw's Punch House, opened in 1738.

The Peveril of the Peak

This historic pub escaped demolition in the early 1980s and in 1988 was named among the 100 best city centre pubs in Britain. Needless to say, the 'Pev' features in the 1989 *'Good Beer Guide'*.

It has stood on Great Bridgewater Street for more than 160 years and is listed as a place of historic and architectural interest. This was mainly because of the pub's ornate wood work, the tiles and fascinating stained glass.

The hostelry was opened in 1830 by an ex-coach driver on the London route called Grundy; he named it after his coach. Rumours suggest that the ghost of a man haunt the place following his being trampled to death on the site by a stage-coach horse. Following refurbishment in 1986, beautifully restored stained glass and a timber bar canopy was installed. Customers may keep an eye open for the ghost as they quaff Websters and Wilsons beers in a friendly and pleasant environment.

The Shakespeare

This popular pub in Fountain Street, behind Lewis's, possesses an interesting history. A tavern has stood on this site since 1771 and the existing Tudor-style building was erected in 1928 from the shell of a pub called 'The Shambles' which had been dismantled in Chester and transported to Manchester.

The area has featured prominently in the eating and drinking habits of Manchester's populace. There used to be an oatmeal market in Fountain Street and, at the junction of this road and York Street the 'George and Dragon' provided some good ale.

It is suggested that the 'Shakespeare' is haunted by the ghost of a girl who died there over 100 years ago. The duties of this kitchen maid included lighting and extinguishing candles in the tavern, but unfortunately one night she accidentally set fire to herself. Running to seek assistance, she fell down the stairs and was killed. An alternative version is that the girl was attacked and raped by a chef, who was later hanged from a beam in the tavern. The rope marks are still visible and rumours indicate that this ghost also haunts the 'Shakespeare'.

The Oxnoble

Occupying a prominent corner of Liverpool Road, this pub has close associations with neighbouring Castlefield. The Potato Wharf reflects the trade in vegetables and the Oxnoble was a type of Norfolk potato popular in 18th century Lancashire. Substantial changes were instituted in 1986 when the pub was re-designed to provide a lounge, principal room and games room at the rear. Visitors can enjoy good lunchtime food plus Chester's mild and bitter on hand pumps.

The Lass-O'-Gowrie

This Charles Street hostelry, formerly known as 'George the Fourth', is well worth visiting. First licensed in 1824, its name derives from a popular Scottish song. The 'Lass O' Gowrie' has been a Chester's house for some time and in 1983 it started brewing its own beer - a pleasant bitter which may be consumed on the premises.

Suburban Pubs

Ancoats

Regulars at the 'Cheshire Cheese', Oldham Road may wish to know that the pub began selling beer in 1823. A century later it came under the auspices of Taylor's Eagle Brewery and today it is a John Smiths house.

Great Ancoats Street of yester-year was a delightful place for tipplers who could enjoy thirty or so pubs as long ago as the 1790s between Oldham Road and Palmerston Street. Latterly, many of these watering holes have vanished and only a handful remain, such as the 'Scotch Heifer', the 'Ancoats', 'Kings Arms', and the 'Cotton Tree'. The last two were listed in an 1811 directory when the 'Cotton Tree' was a brewhouse with a nine barrel capacity.

Pollard Street and Every Street boasted a number of interesting pubs, including the 'Fire Brigade Inn' inaugurated in 1865 and demolished in 1975. The 'River Inn', Palmerston Street traces its origins to 1861

Recipient of several acclamations, the 'Pev' has stood on Great Bridgewater Street for over 160 years.

The Bard looks down on customers entering the pub named after him on Fountain Street.

It is difficult to imagine that this was a lock-up for Manchester criminals.

Occupying a prominent site on Liverpool Road, the 'Oxnoble's' title is derived from a type of potato.

Home-brewed beer drunk in a friendly atmosphere. What more could you want at the 'Lass-O'-Gowrie'?

when it was owned by Cronshaw's Alexandra Brewery, Hulme. It later became a Groves and Whitnall house.

Ardwick

In this area one has to refer to the 'Church' facing Ardwick Green Park. This compact place sells Wilsons beer and appetising meals and is a popular haunt for business people at lunchtime. Two neighbouring pubs of note are the 'George and Dragon', which was first licensed in 1758, although the present building dates from 1871, and the 'Minshull Arms', Downing Street, first licensed in 1763.

Blackley

Lovers of good beer and historic taverns ought to explore this suburb. The deeds of the 'Grove', Rochdale Road, may be traced to the late 18th century. This pub was owned by a number of breweries including Stopfords, the Palatine Bottling Company and Wilsons. The nearby 'White Lion' is 180 years old and is reputed to be haunted, while the 'New White Lion' can trace its ancestry to the 1730s. It was in 1858 that the 'Red Lion' commenced business and once again it came under the jurisdiction of a number of breweries such as Stopfords, the Palatine Bottling Company and Walker and Homfray Limited. Following modifications in the mid-1980s the 'Red Lion' became a Chef and Brewer establishment.

Burnage

This district has never been famous for its wide selection of pubs but there are some worthy of attention. Locals imbibe in the 'Victoria', 'Mauldeth', 'Farmers Arms' and the 'Old Bull'. This last spot was originally a terraced house where Hardy's Ales were sold. During the early 1900s, a larger building was constructed and it is found today adjacent to Kingsway.

The 'Milestone', Burnage Lane is relatively new, opening its doors in August 1986. Built of second-hand bricks it contains an up-market vault and split-level lounge. Customers are tempted by hot lunch-time

54

Once a brewhouse with a nine barrel capacity, the 'Cotton Tree' stands on Great Ancoats Street.

meals, Banks's mild and bitter together with Hanson's Black Country bitter.

Chorlton

Examples of places to have a tipple are the 'Horse and Jockey', the 'Feathers' and, of course, the 'Southern'. This large rambling pub was altered in 1987 to accommodate customers who wished to dine in addition to sampling Boddington's beers. It is likely that a pub belonging to Holts will open in Chorlton during 1989.

Chorlton-on-Medlock

A trip to this district will reveal several notable pubs with long histories. The 'Kings Arms', Helmshore Walk and the 'Church Inn' on Lower Cambridge Street are two instances of older hostelries dating from 1844 and 1852 respectively. It is probable that the 'Church' acquired its name from the nearby All Saints' Church in Grosvenor Square. The imposing 'Plymouth Grove Hotel' is a huge Boddington's house first licensed in 1872 and is popular with locals, university students and office workers.

Didsbury

The 'Royal Oak' specialises in Marston's ales which can be quaffed along with its famous cheese or paté ploughman's lunch. Customers have a wide choice of different cheeses from the UK and Europe. The 'Gateway' occupies a prominent position at Parrswood and is one of Hyde's largest houses. Re-opened in 1988 after extensive alterations, this pub has retained its wood panelling and is a commodious meeting place for locals. Examples of other Didsbury pubs include the 'Station', the 'Old Cock' and the 'Albert'.

Gorton

This district offers a fair selection of pubs and the 'Gorton Mount' on Mount Road serves as an example of a Boddington's house. Among public houses on Hyde Road, one can refer to the 'Waggon and Horses' which was refurbished in 1987, selling Holt's mild and bitter at a reasonable price in pleasant surroundings. The nearby 'Nelson' is now a Wilsons pub and was formerly a Manchester Brewery property. This company was formed in 1888 and sold its famous 'Silver Vatted' ales and Milk Stout at the 'Nelson' and elsewhere. Based in Broadie Street, Ardwick, it was later acquired by Wilsons. The 'Longsight' is a Banks's pub near Belle Vue with a traditional vault and large lounge. Opened in the early 1980s, it is popular with locals and passing trade alike.

Levenshulme

Levenshulme, on the southern side of Manchester, has a number of interesting pubs. Older residents may remember the 'Cheshire Cheese' which stood on Stockport Road, an Issott's Brewery house acquired by Wilson's in 1903. Ardwick-based Issot's had 35 beerhouses, plus a number of fully licensed houses and over a dozen shops.

The 'Horse Shoe' on Chapel Street was owned by Joseph Worrall's Brewery of Stockport until 1896, when Wilsons acquired this pub and 18 more.

The 'Polygon' on Barlow Road was formerly a Clarke's house and today it sells real ale in the form of Boddington's mild and bitter. Not too far away, one discovers the 'Blue Bell' standing on a site some 700 years old, with a pub perhaps dating back some 400 years. Documents of the governing body of Levenshulme indicate that the 'Blue Bell' was their meeting house, the kitchen having the nickname 'The House of Lords'. Construction began on new premises in 1935, following the demolition of the older structure which was supposed to have been visited by Dick Turpin.

The 'Sidings' on Broom Lane is a relatively new pub, opening in 1987, taking its name from a railway coal yard. The 'Sports' on Stockport Road is the new name given to the 'Pack Horse' whose 1907 building replaced that of the original inn, first licensed in 1507. Local children have had considerable fun on the mounting stone which used to stand in front of the pub and is now located at the side. This weather-

The 'Pack Horse' building dates from 1907.

Standing defiantly on Plymouth Grove, the 'Plym' sells Boddingtons beer.

Stockport Road, Levenshulme in the early 1900s. The 'Cheshire Cheese' was acquired by Wilsons in 1903. Advertisements are a reminder of the days when the Evening Chronicle and the 'Manchester Boot Company' were household names.

beaten block of Flintshire granite used to assist travellers in mounting their horses. Older drinkers will remember the interior of the 'Pack Horse' with its ten scenes from Shakespearian plays. Measuring 56 inches long and 2½ feet wide the tiles were made from Royal Doulton china and came from the old Clarence Hotel in Piccadilly when it was demolished.

A glimpse of the Gentlemen's Concert Hall in 1897. Some advertisers are still with us today.

June 1940 at the junction of Deansgate and Quay Street as a lady in a shawl (right) walks towards the Opera House whose sign is visible. The corner shop is requesting clothing for war refugees.

8. The Arts

One of the first theatres in Manchester was located in Marsden Street between 1753 and 1775. The Theatre Royal had its base in Spring Gardens, first opening in 1775. Destroyed by fire in 1790, it was rebuilt and used until 1807 when a new Theatre Royal replaced it as the principal theatre in Manchester. A typical box seat would cost 4s, a Pit seat 2s and the Gallery 1s.

A society for Gentlemen's Concerts was founded in the late 18th century by a group of musicians who initially met in a building on Fountain Street. In 1831, the society moved to new premises at the junction of Peter Street and Lower Mosley Street.

Accommodation was provided for 1,000 people who were offered a variety of classical performances. The People's Concert Hall catered for those preferring a music hall atmosphere and this stood adjacent to the Gentleman's Concert Hall. Both places were demolished in 1898 to make way for the Midland Hotel.

Manchester abounds in a variety of theatres and cinemas, with the Opera House on Quay Street opening as the 'New Theatre' in 1912, designed by Farquharson, Richardson and Gill. The Royal Exchange Theatre is found in the Royal Exchange building (1914-21), and provides a host of attractions including plays and mid-day concerts.

The Cornerhouse on Oxford Street is a lively centre for the visual arts, presenting a varied programme of workshops, debates and films in three cinemas. The Royal Northern College of Music's vast range of skills and productions vary from an evening for double bass to seasons of opera.

To provide further insight into Manchester's theatres three are examined in some detail - the Palace, Forum and Library Theatres.

The Palace Theatre

The curtain first went up on Whit Monday, May 18th, 1891 in a building which had cost its owners £40,500. The ballet 'Cleopatra' from the London Empire was the first performance provided for

Scene from 'Guys and Dolls' performed at the Palace.
Foreground, left to right: Lulu *(Miss Adelaide)*, Norman Rossington *(Nathan Detroit)*, Betsy Brantley *(Sarah)*, Clarke Peters *(Sky Masterson)*.

Palace Theatre queues for the Covent Garden Opera Company, February 1953. 'Willoughby's' pub/restaurant was a popular haunt of theatre-goers.

Do you remember when people queued like this? Some of this crowd had waited all night in order to book for the 1949 Danny Kaye Show.

Manchester theatre-goers, who were offered seats priced from 6d to 4s. Subsequent performances included more ballets and several variety shows amongst whose stars were Charlie Chaplin, Harry Lauder and George Robey. The opening of the New Theatre or Opera House in 1921 forced the Palace to renew itself and there followed extensive refurbishment over a seven month period of closure.

After the First World War more musicals and revues took over from the weekly variety format as renowned actors like Jack Buchanan, Sybil Thorndike and Jessie Matthews trod the boards at the Palace. The advent of the 'talkies' in the 1930s forced theatres to fight for a place in the entertainment business. Crowd-pullers at the Palace included Laurence Olivier, Noel Coward, Charles Laughton and John Mills. Popular radio stars also graced the theatre, particularly in the 1940s when Henry Hall, Vic Oliver, Max Miller, Tommy Trinder and many more gave memorable performances. From America came Laurel and Hardy (1947) and Danny Kaye (1949), while Ivor Novello's *'Dancing Years'* and *'King's Rhapsody'* assured the Palace of an impressive annual profit.

Changing tastes in entertainment brought diverse talents in the 1950s as opera, rock n'roll and plays were shown to the public. The next decade saw *'Maggie May'* and *'Pickwick'* playing to the Manchester audiences who were also able to see several pantomimes in the theatre.

In January 1978, the Palace was bought by the civil engineering and construction company, Norwest Holst who announced details of an impressive scheme to refurbish and renovate the theatre. Reconstruction of the Palace lasted practically three years and cost £3m. as transformation took place backstage and in the seating areas.

Some older Manchester residents will remember 'Willoughby's' next door to the Palace. Like so many places where one could drink (M.S.G., 'Rowntrees', Spring Gardens, etc) 'Willoughby's' has vanished. It was purchased during the rebuilding of the theatre to allow for the extension of bars in the stalls and circle levels.

The reconstructed and extended Manchester Palace has the largest stage and the most sophisticated facilities of any theatre outside London. It is truly the flagship of British provincial theatres.

The Library Theatre and Forum Theatre

The famous theatre under the Central Library was built in 1934 and during the War the BBC used it as a studio. The Manchester Corporation Act of 1946 allowed the Libraries Committee to extend the use of the theatre and then the Art Council's help was obtained to use the theatre for dramatic productions.

Between 1947 and 1952 several companies occupied the theatre as personalities like Tony Britton, Diane Cilento, Joan Miller and Harry H. Corbett trod the boards. The success of the theatre encouraged the Libraries Committee to start its own repertory company and so Peter Lambert was appointed Artistic Director in 1952. In that year, the first production of the Library Theatre Resident Company opened with Oscar Wilde's, *'The Importance of Being Earnest'*.

David Scase became Director of Productions and under his direction the Theatre grew to a position of national prominence.

1971 brought the launch of the 483 seat Forum Theatre at the Civic Centre, Wythenshawe, with John Hale's *'Lorna and Ted'*, performed by the newly-named Library Theatre Company and directed by David Scase. The Forum provided the company with a larger audience plus a technically superior venue. The more spacious backstage areas, modular construction of the stage and hydraulic apron all gave directors and designers greater freedom and flexibility.

Today all costumes, props and sets for both theatres are built at the Forum workshops. Offices are split between the two theatres with the production, design and technical staff at the Forum, while the directors and administrative personnel are based at the Central Library. The original plan was for the Library Theatre Company to run the two theatres in tandem, each play showing for three weeks in one before moving to the other for a further three weeks. However, it became apparent that it would be better to offer separate programmes and, consequently, from 1975 the two theatres developed their own artistic policies, basically involving a four-week repertory system.

The Library Theatre Company produces some 16 plays each year (eight at each theatre), employing over one hundred full-time staff at the height of the season.

Recent premières at both the Library and Forum Theatres include *'Roll on Four O'clock'* by Colin Welland, *'When the Actors Come'* by Don Taylor, and *'The House that Jack Built'* written by Alan Meadows.

Museums and Art Galleries

Manchester provides an interesting selection of museums and galleries to cater for a variety of tastes.

The Police Museum, Newton Street gives an insight into uniforms, equipment and even cells of yesterday, and there is a first class selection of books and old photographs on display. The Greater Manchester Fire Service Museum in Rochdale offers much for those interested in fire appliances from the city's early days.

For public transport enthusiasts the Museum of Transport, Boyle Street Cheetham Hill is an essential place to visit. It houses one of the largest collections of lorries and buses in this country and contains over 60 vehicles in 14 liveries of the buses which were amalgamated to form Greater Manchester Transport. Nearby is the Jewish Museum, a converted synagogue with a marvellous display of Anglo-Jewish life in Britain.

The Castlefield Gallery opened in 1984 and is run by young practising artists. Here children and adults are encouraged to participate in regular workshops.

Manchester Museum

Standing amidst the University buildings on Oxford Road, Manchester Museum was voted Museum of the Year in 1987 by the *'Illustrated London News'*. It accommodates an impressive collection of rocks, fossils, animals, plants and the works of man in ancient and modern times, particularly of Eqyptian and Japanese origin. Renowned for its collection of Egyptian mummies, the museum also provides fascinating displays of Greek and Roman coins. There is an interesting vivarium, plus an aquarium.

Both the Botany and Egyptology galleries were completely renovated between 1985 and 1988 and this in turn has led to a rise in the number of visitors.

Recent improvements include the refurbishment in the Mammoth Gallery. The lively displays will certainly dispel any preconceived ideas of museums housing dull collections of artefacts from the past.

Museum of Science and Industry

One of the largest industry museums in Europe, it tells the story of Greater Manchester, the world's first industrial area. As part of the Castlefield's Urban Heritage Park, the museum provides a variety of new exhibits, working machines and a Science Centre. It has a large collection of working steam engines and houses the Air and Space Gallery where an AVRO Shackleton with its 120 feet wing span is the centre of the display. In fact, 1988 was the 60th anniversary of a history making flight, and this event was celebrated at the Air and Space Museum. It was in 1928 that a biplane made in the city became the first aircraft to fly from England to Australia and the museum's Avro Avian single-engined plan is similar to the one in which test pilot Bert Hinkler made his flight in 1928. The aircraft on display was built in the same year at Avro's Newton Heath works.

One of the more unusual exhibitions of recent years was one in 1988 which charted the history of the city's sewage system. The exhibition included walk-through sewers of the 1830s, complete with an authentic and pungent aroma!

The building

The actual structure offers much to admire. When the goods depot was finally shut in 1975, Great Manchester Council started on the redevelopment and restoration of the passenger station and warehouses. This accommodates the Museum of Science and it was opened to the public in 1983.

Today's visitor may browse among exhibits in the Power Hall, look at the 1830 station building or examine displays depicting the textile industry.

Some of the many exhibits on show at the Museum of Science and Industry.

An example of an aircraft at the Museum of Science and Industry.

Cobbles and tram lines feature in this 1903 look at the City Art Gallery.

A view of the Art Gallery in the 1980s - little has changed over the years.

City Art Gallery and Atheneum

Built by Sir Charles Barry for the Royal Institution of Manchester the Art Gallery was begun in 1825. A Grecian style building featuring a portico of six Ionic columns with pediment, the Art Gallery is a rather sombre structure at the junction of Mosley Street and Princess Street.

Visitors are greeted by an impressive entrance and staircase hall as they go in search of work by Stubbs, Turner, Wilson, Gainsborough and Constable. These are on display together with sculpture and decorative arts.

Barry's work is again observed in the adjacent Atheneum. Dating from 1837, it exhibits a portal with Tuscan columns, plus some interesting pedimented windows.

Whitworth Art Gallery

Standing in Whitworth Park, the Art Gallery is the home of the biggest collection of international textiles outside London. Drawings and watercolours represent the work of a number of artists, including Lowry and Warhol, and visitors can also examine work by Turner and Blake.

Situated approximately $1^{1}/_{2}$ miles from the city centre, the Whitworth Art Gallery provides numerous displays and exhibitions such as Eduardo-Paolozzi's *Sculptures from a Garden*, and *Relief Printing*, together with the famous May Fair held every other year to raise money for the Gallery.

A major appeal was launched in 1988 to mark the centenary of the art gallery. The aim was to build an extension to the main building on the north side of Denmark Road.

The inscription 'For the advancement and diffusion of knowledge' appears over the windows of the Atheneum.

A pyramid roof is a feature of the University's high tower.

9. Education

During the early 1800s, Sunday Schools were the only educational establishments in Manchester apart from Chetham's Hospital and Manchester Grammar School. The Mechanics' Institute was founded in 1824 in what is now St. Peter's Square, offering educational possibilities to ordinary working people. In 1870 an Education Act provided a restricted elementary education which was obligatory. The 19th century heralded considerable advancements in Higher Education when Owens College opened in 1851, moving to its present site in 1873 at a time when post-elementary education was progressing well in the city.

Manchester High School for Girls was established in 1874 and similar Institutions opened to cater for the more academic children aged eleven years and over, both Catholic and non-Catholic. The Central Schools of the early 1900s provided capable Manchester adolescents with a worthwhile education and the 1944 Act brought about the end of all-age schools.

A system of grammar, secondary modern and technical schools evolved and this gave way to comprehensive education in Manchester's state schools in 1967, with Catholic schools following ten years later.

The late 1980s have witnessed interesting developments in Manchester's educational system, where there are some 30 secondary and 142 primary schools.

Higher Education is provided in a number of establishments, including the University, UMIST, the Polytechnic and the Royal Northern College of Music (financed jointly by the cities of Manchester and Salford, Cheshire County Council and Lancashire County Council).

In this chapter, some of the city's more famous schools and places of higher learning are examined.

63

Chetham's

A college school stood on the present site until its dissolution in 1547. The Earl of Derby acquired the buildings ten years later. They were sequestrated by the Government, following the court martial and execution of James, Earl of Derby for his part in the Civil War in 1651. Humphrey Chetham had been negotiating with the Earl of Derby and his agents to buy the collegiate buildings since the late 1640s. He left instructions in his will in 1653 for their purchase to found a school for forty impoverished boys who were to be educated and clothed from the ages of six to 14. The founder stipulated that the school should be made up of six pupils from Salford, ten from Bolton-le-Moors, five from Turton, three from Droylsden, 14 from Manchester and two from Crumpsall. On attaining the age of 14 years, the boys were supplied with two cloth suits and put into apprenticeships. Mr. Chetham also allowed for a library in his institution, providing £200 for this purpose.

In subsequent years, Chetham's school provided choristers for the cathedral and later assumed grammar school status. On becoming an independent school in 1969, Chetham's catered for young musicians of both sexes who obtained entry by audition. The historic collegiate buildings, 15th century refectory and library in the old dormitory wing are still used today. Chetham's is synonymous with music, whilst its free library, comprising over 70,000 volumes is a noted resource.

The Manchester Grammar School

Little is known of the school's founder, Hugh Oldham, Bishop of Exeter. He was a Lancashire man determined to keep education abreast of current trends and developments. With this in mind he founded the school in 1515.

His original schoolhouse lasted for over 250 years and was pulled down to make way for a larger building. Erected in Long Millgate during 1776, this was often referred to as Lawson's School after the High Master, Charles Lawson, whose statue can be seen on the north wall of Manchester Cathedral. The big increase in numbers of pupils, which came after the introduction of fee-payers in the 1860s, necessitated an increase in accommodation. Consequently, a building

This impressive UMIST entrance is found on Sackville Street.

Cricket at Chetham's is played in the school grounds in the early 1900s. Boys and teachers are wearing hats.

Chetham's is a Grade I listed building.

The dining hall at Chetham's in the 1950s.

A wall plaque in Long Millgate marks the original location of Manchester Grammar School.

BUILDING OF ARCHITECTURAL
OR HISTORIC INTEREST
GRADE I
CHETHAM'S HOSPITAL
MANOR HOUSE OF THOMAS DE LA WARRE
GIVEN TO THE COLLEGIATE CHURCH
(NOW CATHEDRAL) IN 1421. IN 1653
HUMPHREY CHETHAM FOUNDED A
SCHOOL AND A FREE PUBLIC
LIBRARY. BECAME A MUSIC
SCHOOL IN 1969.

THE MANCHESTER GRAMMAR SCHOOL

THIS PLAQUE MARKS THE ORIGINAL SITE OF THE MANCHESTER GRAMMAR SCHOOL
ON WHICH FOR MORE THAN FOUR CENTURIES SUCCESSIVE GENERATIONS OF BOYS WERE EDUCATED

THE SCHOOL WAS FOUNDED IN 1515 BY HUGH OLDHAM, BISHOP OF EXETER,
WHOSE ARMS APPEAR ABOVE, AND REMAINED HERE WITHOUT INTERRUPTION UNTIL 1931,
WHEN THE SCHOOL WAS TRANSFERRED TO ITS PRESENT SITE AT RUSHOLME.

was put up in 1870 on the side of Chetham's gateway (this later became a Teacher Training College).

In 1877, the second school built by Lawson was pulled down and a new structure appeared, set at an angle to the 1870 school. Classrooms occupied the first two floors, while the Classical Sixth Form and Library were located in a room in the Tower. The 1870 and 1880 buildings were joined at first floor level by a glass-sided stone bridge, which almost totally hid the 15th century gateway to Chetham's Hospital.

In 1924, there were 1160 boys in the school at a time when Inspectors had suggested the city centre location and absence of playing fields was inadequate, and that alternative premises should be sought.

As a result, the foundation stone on the Rusholme site was laid in 1929 and two years later the school came together in its new home. During the War, the gym was used as a barrage balloon factory. The post-war period brought huge debts for the Governors. This problem was partially alleviated when Manchester Education Committee bought the 1870 buildings in the Long Millgate area.

During 1953 the Refectory was converted to the principal base for the Biology Department and six years later the ground floor of the Physics Department was provided by a grant from the Industrial Fund. Various donations and appeals have resulted in a number of improvements including the Masters' Common Room, 1972. Today's school stands in 28 acres and boasts many facilities including two language laboratories, squash courts, a gymnasium, indoor swimming pool and a micro-computer laboratory. In 1969 the school became independent.

Prominent Manchester Grammar old boys include Lord Sieff and Lord Marks representing the commercial world, playwrights Robert Bolt and Stanley Houghton. John Ogden and Anthony Goldstone are prominent world class pianists. Examples of MPs who studied at Manchester Grammar School were Frank Allaun (Labour), Tom Normanton (Conservative), and Lord Winstanley, formerly Dr. Winstanley (Liberal).

The inscription, 'Schola Mancuniensis 1870' appears over the door of the 1870 Manchester Grammar School building.

It is 1907 in Eagle Street, Smithfield Market where traders queue for produce.

This 1904 view of Scholes Street is from Tib Street. Spratt's animal food is certainly promoted by the shop on the left.

10. Commerce and Industry

The once popular image of Manchester as a place of satanic mills has now been dispelled. The city is recognised as a financial centre and the base for numerous service industries. Modern office blocks and conversion of Victorian buildings are at the heart of the city's commercial and industrial life.

Of course, Manchester has been at the forefront of commercial trends for centuries. Its first bank opened in 1771. Before that, 1729 brought the establishment of the Exchange. A commercial society founded in 1794 later became the Manchester Chamber of Commerce.

A predominant trading interest was cotton, assisted by the moist climate which helped in weaving. Furthermore an abundant supply of soft water proved invaluable in the finishing process. The proximity of coal fields and a network of canals and roads also contributed to the success of the cotton industry.

In 1928, cotton goods represented one fifth of the total exports from Great Britain but gradually artificial products damaged cotton's popularity.

Manchester has made several important contributions to commerce. In the early 1800s, it played a major rôle in the electoral reform agitation that led to the Reform Act of 1832 and the Anti-Corn Law League which led to the repeal of the Corn Laws in 1846. Today the headquarters of the large Co-operative Wholesale Society are found in the city.

Manchester's markets have long been the principal source of fresh produce for trades in and around the city. In fact there was an open market on the site of Shudehill's Smithfield Market as far back as 1821.

The commerce of yesterday is reflected in a variety of buildings: including St. James's Buildings, Oxford Street; the Corn Exchange; the Refuge, Oxford Road; and Upper Campfield Market, whose cast iron and glass market halls house a number of businesses.

Manchester has, of course, been the home of many famous manufacturers, including Beyer-Peacock Limited, whose railway locomotives were (and some still are) found throughout the world from as far afield as the East Indian Railways and South African Railways. William Timpson left Kettering to open his first two boot and shoe shops in Oldham Street and Stretford Road in 1870. Again, Rolls of Rolls Royce built his first cars in Hulme, while Crossley's Motor Works had a home in Manchester. Alliott Vernon Roe (Avro) manufactured planes in Great Ancoats Street and Sebastian de Ferranti, who developed the alternator, made his home in Manchester.

Shops in Manchester

Markets in Manchester were found in several locations, near the Old Shambles, Miller Street and a meal and flour market was held in a building also used as a Methodist Chapel in High Street. Fennel Street was the home of the corn market. There was a shoe market in Withy Grove in the early 1800s and cotton goods were sold in the vicinity of Market Street.

Shops gradually replaced market stalls in the 19th century along Market Street and Deansgate, one of the first major shops belonging to Kendal, Milne and Faulkner. Initially concentrating on silks and drapery, the company expanded and built a new shop in Deansgate in 1870. By this time there were other larger department stores in the city, typified by Lewis's (1867), with a new building constructed in 1880. Perhaps one of the most important people to open a shop in Manchester was Michael Marks. His success is legendary and his story is told below.

Marks and Spencer

Michael Marks was a Russian immigrant who began his working life as a market trader in Leeds in 1884. He established a network of market stalls in the north of England, famous for their notice, "Don't ask the price, it's a penny."

99 Stockport Road, Levenshulme in 1915 was a Marks and Spencer Penny Bazaar which remained on this site until its closure in 1938.

Customers at Marks and Spencer's Shop, Levenshulme are informed that admission is free.

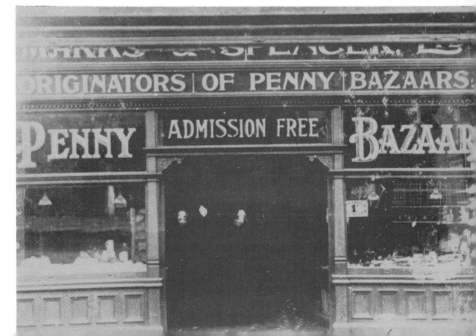

Lewis's, Market Street 1940 asks customers to support the war effort.

Moving to Manchester in 1894, Marks opened his first shop in Cheetham Hill Road, then went into partnership with Leeds book-keeper Tom Spencer. In 1896, premises sprung up at 65 Stretford Road where they remained until closure in 1933. Following the success of this venture, a Marks and Spencer store occupied a site between 1897 and 1899 at Campfield market, Liverpool Road. It was about this time that a further shop made its début at 60 Oldham Street. Occupying 1400 square feet, this shop carried on trading until 1925.

Other Marks and Spencer outlets were on Regent Road, Salford and 99 Stockport Road, Levenshulme. This Penny Bazaar started trading in 1915, occupying 660 square feet and it remained on the busy A6 site until just before the Second World War.

Realising the potential of city centre premises, M & S decided to set up a business at 48-50 Oldham Street, Manchester between a ladies' costume shop and Philip Hart Limited, 'the complete house furnisher'. This business opened in 1925, and was extended and rebuilt four years later.

The shop at 111-117 Market Street was launched in November 1931, occupying a total of 18,000 square feet, and comprising a basement and ground floor. Various extensions took place until 1961 when a new site was acquired at 7-17 Market Street. Once again, extensions were built in 1977, increasing the original 40,000 square feet to 62,700 square feet. During 1978 a first floor link provided further sales areas and the first floor was extended in 1984 to provide some 29,800 square feet.

When next shopping in Marks and Spencer, Manchester, it may be worth considering for a moment the terrific expansion of the business since its early days in 1894 on Cheetham Hill Road.

The Arndale Centre

The popularity of Europe's largest covered shopping complex is shown by recent figures. During the 1987 Christmas period, some 1.5 million people passed through the centre, while the weekly average for 1988/89 is 802,000.

A controversial building at its launch, the bright revitalised Arndale Centre of today has shed its rather bleak image. A £25m.

An interesting look into Marks and Spencer, 48/50 Oldham Street, in 1925 when safety pins were two pennies a bundle.

Natural light in the Arndale Centre has been made possible by replacing part of the roof with glazing.

C & A in 1957 just after the store opened.

The GNR warehouse dominates the Watson Street area of Central Manchester.

transformation involved both the exterior and interior with the atmosphere inside improved by removing parts of the roof and glazing the spaces to let in natural light. Abundant foliage and plants enhance the extra staircases, which now benefit from up dated lighting. The success of this refurbishment is apparent in terms of increased numbers of shoppers and also in the 30 new tenants who arrived within a twelve month period, including major names like 'McDonalds', 'Next' and British Telecom.

Of course, the establishment of the Arndale Centre encouraged several larger departmental stores to more there. One example was C and A whose shop was formerly on Oldham Street. Modernised in 1957, this building was closed down in 1978 upon the opening of a new C & A store in the Arndale Centre.

Warehouses

Manchester's industry and commerce depended largely on vast warehouses scattered throughout the city. Cotton production was encouraged by soft water, a damp climate and proximity to Liverpool. The growth of canal traffic and the boom in the cotton industry led to the construction of warehouses, particularly in the vicinity of the Castlefield Basin. In fact, a directory of the mid 18th century indicates that this area had warehouses owned by cotton manufacturers and companies connected with the corn and salt industries. A dry goods warehouse was built in the basin area by James Brindley in 1778 and some fifty years later a line of warehouses stretched as far as Knott Mill. Still in the Castlefield area, there was a canal warehouse finished in 1829 known as Merchants' Warehouse; today it serves as a good reminder of 19th century architecture. Of course, many warehouses have been demolished over the years for a variety of reasons. However, some still exist like the Victoria and Albert warehouses on Water Street. Recent attention has focussed on the Grocer's Warehouse, restored to its former glory after being rescued from the Manchester Ship Canal Company by the City Council. The previously derelict building was re-opened in 1988 and houses a functional water wheel and hydraulic lifting gear.

73

The Great Northern Railway Company's goods station and warehouse was begun in 1885, the warehouse opening in 1898. A five-storey building measuring 250 feet long and 120 feet wide, this warehouse dominates Watson Street and surrounding areas. The canal and rail traffic encouraged the construction of warehouses adjacent to London Road Station. Four were built between 1857 and 1867. Today the London Warehouse still stands as a memento to Manchester's commerce of yesterday. It is a seven-storey structure, 180 feet square whose huge cast iron columns support massive riveted wrought-iron box-girders.

It is refreshing to know that Manchester's industrial and commercial inheritance is being remembered as warehouses are refurbished and redeveloped. A case in point is Grocer's Warehouse, while the Watt's Warehouse story is told in the account of the Britannia Hotel (see below).

Hotels

Manchester's rôle as a commercial centre encouraged visitors to spend time in the hotels which began to spring up in the 1800s. The Albion Hotel opened in Piccadilly in 1815, closing just over a century later. The Queen's Hotel in Portland Street was designed by Waters, and commenced business in 1845, while the Grand Hotel was ready to receive guests in 1883, following refurbishment of this former warehouse.

Today there are over 70 hotels in Manchester, perhaps the Hotel Piccadilly, the Midland and the Britannia being best known. The Piccadilly Plaza redevelopment scheme has shopping on two levels, offices and, of course, the Hotel Piccadilly, dating from the early 1960s. With 255 bedrooms and seven conference rooms, this is a popular spot for visitors from home and abroad. The restoration and rebuilding of the Midland Hotel and Britannia Hotel will be considered in some detail, since both places have fascinating histories and play a prominent rôle in Manchester's development.

The austere London Warehouse on Ducie Street dates from 1867.

The Midland Hotel in 1949. Behind is Central Station, while the van at the bottom left sports the name of a long disappeared newspaper, 'The Daily Graphic'.

A peaceful spot where time seems to have passed by, the elegant Stanley Room in the Midland Hotel.

The Midland Hotel

Since its inception in 1903, the Midland Hotel has combined unparalleled service with a reputation for excellent cuisine and elegance. Before the building of a hotel, the two acre site contained a high walled garden belonging to a Mr. Cooper, which figures in a contemporary lithograph of the scene of Peterloo in 1821. There then followed the construction of a school and two concert halls (see above) which were demolished to make way for the hotel. The owner of one concert hall, Charles Heywood, resisted the sale but eventually agreed on condition that the Midland Railway Company would incorporate a theatre/concert room of equal size within their new hotel.

The building

Charles Trubshaw designed his six-storey hotel around two wells, with a centre dividing section which supported two giant water tanks housed on the roof. The design called for a steel frame clothed in polished granite and terracotta, and the whole structure cost £1¼ million to build. The Midland Hotel was formally declared open in September 1903, boasting first class facilities typified by Turkish baths in the basement, several shops, including a sub-post office and a telephone next to each bed. Louis XVI décor embellished the reception area and French restaurant. The railway company had done more than just honour their agreement for the replacement for the Gentleman's Concert Hall, since there was now an 800-seat theatre with imposing support pillars for ceilings and balconies. It had its own separate entrance facing Central Station. The curtain came down for the last time in 1922 and later three floors of modern bedrooms were constructed between the floor and ceiling of the theatre.

Restoration

May 1985 brought the closure of the hotel for total restoration with over 18,000 tonnes of excavation taken away before refurbishment could begin. The developer's brief was clear - preserve the extravagant Edwardian décor and provide the most luxurious of modern accommodation.

75

As a consequence, ornately plastered walls and ceilings such as those in the Trafford restaurant have been retained, while oak and walnut panelling in public rooms have been restored. Stonemasons gave new life to areas of white marble lining corridors and staircases together with the marble pillars supporting the high dome of the Octagon Court.

There were 600 bedrooms when the hotel first opened, and today there are 303 because every spacious room conforms to the high standards of a Holiday Inn Crown Plaza Hotel. All bedrooms now have en suite bathrooms, whereas in the original Midland only 100 rooms had baths.

The hotel forms part of the Manchester central redevelopment programme which covered an area of 26 acres, including the G-Mex exhibition centre. The tradition of excellence is reborn in a setting of Edwardian opulence which provides a complete range of banqueting and conference suites, a ballroom, leisure complex and casino.

The Britannia Hotel

Transformed from a warehouse to a large international hotel, the Britannia commenced business on March 1st, 1982. It rose like a phoenix out of the ashes of the Lancashire cotton industry's most famous warehouse, the S and J Watts Building, which came into existence on 16th March, 1888. This site was once the spot for number 35 Portland Street, a cottage occupied by one Mrs. Monks who was injured at the so-called battle of Peterloo.

The building and the business

The warehouse was the largest building in Manchester devoted to mercantile purposes and cost £100,000 to build between 1857 and 1888. Architects Train and Magnall created a structure 300 feet long, 900 feet deep and over 100 feet high. The style is Venetian, each floor having a different name. The granite base is Egyptian, the third floor Elizabethan, while the fourth floor is based on the Galerie de Glaces at Versailles.

This building of Samuel and John Watts was used for wholesale purposes, the owners buying in bulk from manufacturers and selling in smaller quantities to retailers. The company had 150 representatives who travelled throughout Britain and the world. The firm expanded into manufacturing enterprises with two factories in Manchester, one in Crewe and one in Hazel Grove.

Changes to the building

During the Second World War, incendiaries damaging the main building were dealt with by the warehouse's fire squad. The leader of this intrepid band was Chief Fireman Beckett, who, in 1941, was invested with the Civil Division of the Most Excellent Order of the British Empire.

S and J Watts Company continued until 1960 when it amalgamated and was renamed Cook and Watts, later becoming part of the Courtauld's Group in 1986. During 1973, the warehouse changed hands and in 1979 Britannia Hotels purchased the building.

The hotel

There are 360 bedrooms in this de luxe international hotel, which is one of the busiest in the country. The complex offers 'Saturdays' discotheque and 'Kicks' discotheque, while the Crompton's Restaurant and Cocktail Bar have been created from the shelving and panelling salvaged from an old Victorian shop which used to stand on Cross Street. The Spindles Health Club provides a gymnasium, swimming pool, 15 steam rooms and a sauna, while the hotel has the best in conference, meeting and banqueting facilities.

Purchased from the Receiver, the Watts Warehouse had been empty for approximately seven years and was then in a poor state of repair. Its development as a city centre hotel brought life into this part of Manchester, increased employment prospects and enhanced this stretch of Portland Street.

Brewing

Websters-Wilsons

Since its inception in 1834, Wilsons Brewery has made quite an impact on the drinking habits of people in Manchester and its environs.

The tasteful interior of the modern Midland.

There are 303 luxurious bedrooms in the hotel.

Horse-drawn vehicles mingle with lorries and cars in Portland Street, 1937. The S and J Watts building is the second block from the right.

The Britannia Hotel is 23 bays in length.

The 'Flower Pot' on Red Bank, Manchester was a good example of a pub for locals.

Each floor at the Britannia offers an interesting and varied style of architecture.

A welcome break from unloading barrels in the 1940s.

Samuel Webster came together with Wilsons in 1985 to form a new company. In addition to selling to pubs, the products of this company are sold throughout thousands of free trade outlets in the north, midlands, Scotland and Northern Ireland.

So when did Wilsons Brewery come to Manchester? John Collinson and George Simpson started a brewery in Monsall Lane in 1837 and rented some cottages, later acquiring further property and land in 1850 and 1853. The brewery continued with the Simpson family until its acquisition by Henry Charles Wilson and Thomas Philpott in 1865. By now the brewery occupied premises on the north and west side of Monsall Lane. In 1884 Hubert Malcolm Wilson was made a partner in the business by his father.

Between 1888 and 1890 Hubert acquired the leasehold of 25 licensed houses and the freehold of 22 other licensed premises, including some which are still standing today - the 'New White Lion', Blackley, the 'Lord Nelson', Salford and the 'Millstone', Manchester. Wilsons Brewery Company bought Joseph Worrall's of Stockport in 1896, Jowett, Waterhouse and Company, Oldham, and the property of Cardwell and Company in 1899. This last deal brought 120 licensed houses under Wilsons' control, including the 'City Arms' on Kennedy Street, and the 'Shamrock', Bengal Street. Issott's Ardwick Place Brewery was bought in 1903, along with Kay and Whittaker Ltd, whose pubs included the 'Waggon and Horses', Birch Lane, Longsight, the 'Shakespeare', Fountain Street and the 'White Lion', Withington.

At the outbreak of the First World War, Wilson received its first motor lorries plus a company car - a Fiat Landaulette. After the war the company bought a new Foden steam wagon at a cost of £645.

Acquisitions were still commonplace and in 1925 Alfred Crowther's Brewery was purchased with its 23 pubs. The famous Wilson trademark, the draughtboard, made its début in 1925, the first pub to use the new logo being the 'Blue Bell' in Oldham Road. Wilsons products were advertised on cinema screens for the first time in 1931 and their Wembley Ale appeared in newspaper advertisements in 1934.

During the Second World War, several Wilson houses were damaged or destroyed in the Manchester blitz. This did not deter the brewery from supplying beer to the troops and in 1944 the company provided 936 barrels a month.

Following the war, the firm doubled their number of tied houses by merging with Walker and Homfray's, whose outlets included the 'Albert Inn', Wilmslow Road; the 'Beehive', Petersgate, Stockport; 'Comfortable Gill', King Street West, Stockport; the 'Mauldeth', Kingsway, Burnage and the 'Seymour', Upper Chorlton Road, Chorlton. This last named pub was let to Walker and Homfrays by the Palatine Bottling Company. It was conveyed to Wilsons in 1968.

Wilsons by now was the largest brewery in the area, enjoying terrific success. The Olympic beer was introduced in 1950 but the early years of the decade brought disconcerting news. Post-war development plans meant that old property was to be demolished - in Oldham, for example, 14 Wilson houses had to go, while similar events took place in Mill Street, Ancoats and parts of Hulme. In 1960, Manchester Corporation announced they were looking for Parliamentary powers to build the Mancunian Way and eventually this led to the demise of ten Wilson pubs, including the 'Clarendon'; Oxford Road, the 'Royal Oak', Downing Street and 'Victoria', City Road.

The London-based Watney Mann group assumed control of Wilsons in 1960 and 2000 barrels of Red Barrel were produced a week at Newton Heath. During the 1960s, extensive reorganisation and rebuilding of the Newton Heath brewery.

In the mid-1960s, more clearance orders closed several pubs in Salford, Bury and the city centre. Wilsons took over the Wakefield-based Beverly Brothers and a new company, Watney Mann (North) was established. Four years later Grand Metropolitan acquired Watney Mann in 1972 regional company names reappeared. Once again, the famous draught board sign was in evidence, as beers from the Newton Heath brewery were once more called Wilsons mild and Wilsons bitter.

In 1983 several meetings took place to improve Wilsons' identity and image. A £5m. investment programme included a new tank room facility on the brewery's complex. Later, Fosters draught beer appeared in Wilsons' pubs. Over one hundred premises were refurbished in the mid-1980s.

Pictured here when it was a Walker and Homfray's house, the 'Seymour Hotel' is situated on Upper Chorlton Road.

Some Independent Breweries

The principal independents in Greater Manchester include Hydes, Holt, Boddington's and Robinson. This last brewery is located in Stockport and for further details see the Author's book 'A Portrait of Stockport'. These independents sell real ale in all their pubs and although many Manchester public houses are owned by the Big Seven brewers, it is possible to discover traditional beers in some of their outlets. Manchester and the north-west have more independent brewers than any other area and some of these will be now examined.

Boddington's

The Strangeways brewery dates from 1778 and Boddington's have been in charge since 1853. The company acquired G.R. Clayton brewery and its 17 pubs in 1888. Clarke's brewery was purchased in 1962 giving Boddington's a further 60 outlets in return for their £1,000,000 investment. Boddington's bought Swales Naval Brewery of Hulme in 1971, adding a further 38 pubs and six off-licences to its list of hostelries.

More recently Boddington's took control of Oldham Brewery and the Liverpool based Higson's brewery (1985). The first named company was subsequently closed in 1988 when beer production moved to Strangeways. In that year the company carried out major reorganisation, including the closure of its Oldham brewery. It also stepped up its investment in hotels, catering and leisure with a total of 50 'Henry's Table' restaurants planned for 1990. Ewart Boddington, chairman for almost 19 years, retired from the chair at the end of 1988 but remains with the company as a non-executive director.

Holt's

Famed for its low priced products this company tends to have most of its pubs in north Manchester, Eccles and Prestwich. The brewery is now looking further afield for outlets, exemplified by the 'The Sidings' on Broom Lane, Levenshulme.

The stately entrance to the Refuge seen from the courtyard in the early 1950s.

Holt's is proud of the strength of its beers and a recipe which has not changed for 30 years. Town water has been used for brewing since 1969 and malt is supplied mainly from Yorkshire and counties in the south-east of England.

If you fancy a drink in traditional surroundings where beer is sensibly priced why not try the 'Derby Brewery Arms' on Cheetham Hill Road, the 'Grafton', Chorlton-on-Medlock or Yate's Wine Lodge, High Street, Manchester.

Hyde's

Hyde's Anvil brewery owns some 50 tied houses selling real ale. The Moss Lane East company provides a bitter, best mild and the famous Anvil Strong Ale. Examples of city centre pubs where a good pint is always available would be the 'Jolly Angler', Ducie Street and the 'Dutton' on Park Street, not far from Victoria Station.

Banking and Insurance

Refuge Assurance

Once a familiar landmark for commuters and visitors, the Refuge building in Oxford Street no longer houses the headquarters of Refuge Assurance. After more than one hundred and thirty years spent almost entirely in the centre of Manchester, and nearly a century in Oxford Street, the organisation moved to Wilmslow in 1987.

When the company ran out of space about a century ago and just 30 years after its inception, the directors looked around for a central site in Manchester. In spite of extensions to the Corporation Street headquarters, there was insufficient room for a progressive company. Consequently, in 1890 the directors paid £21,000 for an 1,800 square yard parcel of land at the corner of Whitworth Street and Oxford Street. The eminent Victorian architect Alfred Waterhouse was engaged to design a new building and his name was well known through projects as diverse as Manchester Town Hall, the city's Assize Courts, plus Leeds, Liverpool and Manchester Universities.

By the summer of 1895 Refuge number one building was completed and occupied. It was one of Waterhouse's most ornately Gothic works, whose symmetry and elegance has continued to draw admiring glances from passers-by. This structure was a good example of how terracotta could be employed to combat the grime of industrial pollution that settled on Manchester's Victorian buildings.

Furbished with richly-glazed decorative tiles the interior was illuminated by gas mantles while coal- fired boilers provided central heating until the 1930s.

Within 10 years of opening, number one building was fully occupied and so Waterhouse's son Paul was called on to design a second structure. This featured some spectacular designs, including the soaring 217 foot clock tower. Building number three was completed in 1935 to a design by Stanley Birkett and typifies the changing employer-worker relationship of the times. It had a huge sprung-floored basement hall plus a stage complex which doubled as a dining room and recreation area.

During the Second World War hundreds of tons of girders were fixed in the basement to provide a secure shelter for the 1300 members of staff in the event of German bombing raids.

A source of inspiration and strength, the Refuge building ignored German bombs and dominated a desolate landscape in the 1960s when inner city rebuilding took place.

The Wilmslow-based Refuge headquarters started as a skeleton of concrete girders, later clad in 600,000 handmade bricks to give a tasteful mellow appearance to the building. The large scale three-day move from Manchester was completed 12 hours ahead of schedule and without the loss of a single document. Oxford Street days are not forgotten, however. One important reminder of yester-year is a 33 feet high war memorial which had stood proudly in the central courtyard on the Manchester site for 65 years. It now looks out from its wooded setting to a man-made lake.

The Midland Bank

A walk round King Street and Spring Gardens will reveal a number of

At 217 feet in height the Refuge clock tower provides some admirable views of Manchester and its environs.

The immutable landmark of the Refuge Assurance building on Oxford Street.

Customers in 1935 carried out their transactions in this magnificent Banking Hall.

important banks which control so much of Manchester's business. One of these is the Midland Bank.

Background

The Midland Bank's link with Manchester can be traced back to the formation of the banking firm of Robertson, Fraser and Company in 1863. Based in the High Street, it was converted into a limited liability company and renamed the Manchester Joint Stock Bank in 1873. Its head office was removed to King Street in 1879 and over the next 12 years the Bank opened nine branches in the Manchester area. The Bank, together with its branches and staff, became part of Midland Bank in 1892 and from that point provided the care of Midland's expanding business in Manchester.

The building

The Bank's property in King Street had all the advantages of an island site. In August 1928, a new design was drawn up by Sir Edwin Lutyen's, Whinney Son and Austen Hall. Their brief was to provide both a spacious banking hall and sufficient accommodation for the branch staff, the Manchester branch of the Bank's Trust Company and the Bank's existing tenants.

Lutyens, of course, was a successful architect of public buildings and monuments and his introduction to the Midland Bank came directly through his friend and client Reginald McKenna. Throughout Sir Edwin Lutyen's long association with the Midland Bank he was responsible for many buildings and by 1939 the bank's confidence in him was seen in a legacy of distinctive buildings at the heart of the United Kingdom's banking community.

When designing the Manchester bank, Lutyens opted for a tower form of building partly so as to ensure that the new office would not be dwarfed by neighbouring offices of the Manchester Ship Canal Company. The elevation drawings indicated a combination of the classical base, a tall rather plain middle section, carrying four of the eight storeys, and a classical top. Lutyens solved the problem of lighting the upper storeys by creating a deep lighting well in the centre

83

The monolithic Midland just after it commenced business in the mid-1930s.

of the building. But he was not totally responsible for all decisions and one of his main collaborators, Austen Hall had to convince him that Portland stone should be used. Again, Frederick Hyde persuaded Sir Edwin that a granite plinth should feature in the base of the building.

Work was finished in 1929 and some sixty years later this Portland stone edifice asserts itself over younger neighbours.

This 1954 aerial view of Piccadilly reveals the empty area on the left that was to become the site for the Piccadilly Hotel, shops and offices.

A look at Piccadilly Gardens in 1937. The logo MCT on the bus shelters refers to Manchester Corporation Transport Department.

11. Street Scenes of Yesterday

This section will remind many people of the 'good old days' when tram lines and overhead trolleybus wires were the norm. There are views of suburban Manchester and also city centre streets and squares. In some cases, the scene has changed little but in other instances it is hard to visualise that a particular street or square actually looked the way it did. Of course, the change in fashion is shown in these scenes of Manchester and some once famous shops have now vanished.

Enjoy your stroll down memory lane!

Piccadilly

Formerly a clay pit, this part of Manchester did not acquire the name Piccadilly until the early 1800s. The main building was, of course, the Infirmary, which was demolished in 1909 and moved to new premises in Oxford Road. Its city centre site was developed as a garden. Gradually, houses in Piccadilly were replaced by hotels and commercial buildings, with earlier examples including the Albion Hotel at the corner of Oldham Street and the Queen's, constructed in 1845.

Examples of statutes in Piccadilly are one of Sir Robert Peel (1853), Wellington (1856) and a memorial to Queen Victoria (1901). One of the first major post-war developments was the huge Piccadilly Plaza (1960-65) by Covell, Mathews and Partners. It features a podium, first floor shopping piazza, hotel and offices.

Piccadilly has been the terminus for many of Manchester's bus routes and today numerous services operate from here.

Deansgate

Deansgate has always been the approach to Manchester from the south

This bustling Deansgate scene underlines the major drawback of trams. These open-top vehicles are held up by trams in front, and, of course, overtaking is impossible.

Victoria Buildings in 1923 from the Royal Exchange. The two window awnings protect goods on display in Duncan and Foster.

Christmas traffic in Market Street, 1957 gives a good insight into popular vehicles of 30 years ago.

Looking down Oldham Street in 1955 from C and A Modes towards Piccadilly.

and west, connecting the area of the Roman camp to the medieval heart of the town near Chetham's and the old Manchester Grammar School. Deansgate first had half-timbered houses which gave way to brick buildings and Victorian commercial premises. It seems likely it takes its name from the Old English/Old Norse 'dene' meaning a valley and 'gate' which means a road. Older Mancunians may remember Mawson's Buildings, Barton's Buildings and the Grosvenor Hotel which dated from 1879. Today's structures include Royal London House (1904), Elliot House (1878 with a later extension), Kendal Milne and Company, the Halifax Building Society (1983) and John Rylands Library.

The Victoria Buildings

This superb view of the Victoria Buildings dates from 1923 and was taken from the Royal Exchange. The three-sided Victoria Buildings lay in a triangle formed by St. Mary's Gate, Victoria Street and Deansgate. It was built in 1876 on the site of a street called Smithy Door, a section of which had to be cleared in 1837 to allow Victoria Street to be built.

The Victoria Buildings were destroyed in the Blitz, which also brought about the end of a number of businesses on the site, including Duncan and Foster, Courtaulds and several steamship companies.

Market Street

Known originally as Market Stede Lane, this thoroughfare was renamed Market Street in early 1800s. Once a principal route through the centre of Manchester, the area is now pedestrianised. As far back as the 1700s, it was a main way through the centre, a widening programme of the early 1800s resulting in considerable demolition of property.

Oldham Street

This thoroughfare received its name from a local resident, Adam Oldham. Traditionally one of Manchester's popular shopping centres, Oldham Street lost many of its famous shops such as C & A to the Arndale Centre and its immediate vicinity.

The photograph on page 91 of this book shows Oldham Street in 1901 with Boots on the left and Yates's Wine Lodge on the right. Modern Oldham Street still provides a Yates's for shoppers who fancy a quick Australian sherry!

Albert Square

Before the arrival of the Town Hall the district now known as Albert Square comprised many terraced houses and factories together with premises for Manchester Fire Brigade. It became evident in the 1860s that the Town Hall on King Street was too small, so a new one was constructed. The buildings in and around modern Albert Square were mainly back-to-back properties and these were demolished to make the square. It had a memorial to the Prince Consort as its centre-piece. The Albert Memorial was designed by Worthington, while the statue is the work of Matthew Noble. Other statues are Gladstone (1901), Oliver Heywood (1894), John Bright (1891) and the second Bishop of Manchester, James Fraser (1887).

The illustration shows Albert Square in 1895 with the four-year-old statue of Bright on the left of the scene. The fountain no longer exists. The horse-drawn buses from Cheetham Hill and Hightown turned round in Albert Square for their journeys back to the suburbs.

London Road

The sandbags and policeman's satchel for his gas mask indicate the time this photograph was taken. The year was 1940 and the scene provides a useful insight into how Manchester fared in the war years some 50 years ago.

The Police and Fire Station at the junction of Whitworth Street and London Road was designed by Woodhouse, Willoughby and Langham and was built in 1901-6. Occupying a triangular piece of land, the structure consisted of red brick and yellow terracotta with a distinctive tower. In its heyday, it accommodated policemen, firemen and their families together with stables for the fire horses.

When GMC Fire Service opened a new station in Thompson Street,

This gem from the past depicts Albert Square in 1895. John Bright's statue (left) was four years old when this scene was recorded almost one hundred years ago.

1940 outside London Road Police and Fire Station where sandbags act as protection against enemy bombing.

A fireman peeps out of Pollard Street Fire Station in 1906.

Remember the 'Plaza' in Oxford Street? It is January 1st, 1936 and advertisements inform revellers of facilities available.

London Road Fire Station closed. The move took place in 1986 after the old premises had served Manchester for some 85 years.

One of the nearest fire stations to London Road was in Upton Street with a neighbouring station being found at Pollard Street. The latter was built in 1865, closing in 1938 when firemen and their vehicles moved to Withington.

The bus shown in the London Road picture is a Crossley 'Mancunian' featuring Metro-Cammell Crossley B32R bodywork. Built in 1936, the number 33 is going to Romily and Greave.

Oxford Street

Manchester city centre residents could walk via the countryside of Oxford Street to Chorlton in the late 18th century. Gradually, its appearance changed as it assumed the rôle of a business and entertainment centre. The Refuge Assurance Company has already been described, and other examples of commercial architecture included Prince's Buildings and St. James's Buildings.

The original structure of Prince's Buildings dates from 1903, although all that remains today is the façade. Extensive rebuilding has provided many offices in this prime location. St. James's Buildings took three years to construct, opening in 1912. The work of Clegg, Fryer and Penman, this structure features numerous pediments and pilasters.

The Tootal Broadhurst red brick building has dominated Oxford Street since 1898 and is the work of architect Gibbon Sankey.

The Odeon Cinema dates from 1930, while the Plaza (later Tiffany's) was a favourite spot for dancing. The Palace Theatre is also found on Oxford Street and is mentioned elsewhere in this book.

Burnage Lane

This photograph was taken in October 1906 and shows the junction of Burnage Lane and Fog Lane, Burnage. The buildings date from the early 1800s and were cleared in 1930 to provide room for more modern housing. A village smithy stood at the Fog Lane/Burnage Lane junction

The Burnage Lane and Fog Lane junction was a most idyllic spot in 1906.

near the 'Bull Inn'. This was once a terraced cottage where Hardy's Ales were sold.

Albert Road, Levenshulme

The photographer was standing at the junction of Albert Road and Stockport Road in December 1936. Manchester is to his right and Stockport 2^1/$_2$ miles to his left. The sign post was taken down when war started in 1939, so it would not provide useful information for enemy parachutists.

Levenshulme LMS station is just to the right of the bridge, the second station out of London Road on the Manchester-Crewe line. Dating from 1842, Levenshulme North was one of two stations in the suburb, with Levenshulme South located near Station Road (now Crayfield Road). The 'Railway' pub in the illustration can trace its roots to the mid-19th century when it was owned by the Empress Brewery Company. More recently it sold Chester's beer.

Apart from the cobbles and tram lines, little has altered in terms of buildings at this busy junction on the A6.

With his back to the 'Union' pub, the photographer recorded this view of Albert Road, Levenshulme in 1936.

The pub, railway station and bank are still in evidence in the late 1980s.

Two businesses in this 1901 view of Oldham Street are still with us: Yates's Wine Lodge (right) and Boots (left).

Key

1. Victoria Station
2. Chetham's
3. Site of original Manchester Grammar School
4. Cathedral
5. 'Sinclair's'
6. 'Wellington' Inn
7. St. Ann's Church
8. St. Mary's Mulberry St.
9. John Rylands Library
10. Opera House
11. Granada TV
12. Museum of Science and Industry
13. Liverpool Road Railway Station
14. St. Mathew's Sunday School
15. Castlefield
16. 'Oxnoble' Public House
17. Deansgate Railway Station
18. GNR Warehouse
19. G-MEX
20. Free Trade Hall
21. Midland Hotel
22. 'Tommy Ducks' Public House
23. Central Library and Library Theatre
24. Town Hall
25. Albert Square
26. 'Peveril of the Peak' Public House
27. Oxford Road Railway Station
28. BBC Studios
29. 'Lass-o'-Gowrie' Public House
30. Palace Theatre
31. Former London Road Fire Station
32. Piccadilly Railway Station
33. London Warehouse
34. 'Brunswick' Public House
35. Piccadilly Gardens
36. Britannia Hotel
37. China Town
38. Art Gallery
39. Yang Sing Restaurant
40. Midland Bank
41. 'Shakespeare' Public House
42. Arndale Centre